THE MIDDLE EAST IN TURMOIL

TURKEY AND THE U.S.

ALLIANCES, RELATIONS AND DEFENSE COOPERATION

THE MIDDLE EAST IN TURMOIL

Additional books in this series can be found on Nova's website under the Series tab.

Additional E-books in this series can be found on Nova's website under the E-books tab.

DEFENSE, SECURITY AND STRATEGIES

Additional books in this series can be found on Nova's website under the Series tab.

Additional E-books in this series can be found on Nova's website under the E-books tab.

THE MIDDLE EAST IN TURMOIL

TURKEY AND THE U.S.

ALLIANCES, RELATIONS AND DEFENSE COOPERATION

SAMANTHA N. BOOTHE
AND
RYAN HICKMAN
EDITORS

Nova Science Publishers, Inc.
New York

For permission to use material from this book please contact us:
Telephone 631-231-7269; Fax 631-231-8175
Web Site: http://www.novapublishers.com

Additional color graphics may be available in the e-book version of this book.

Library of Congress Cataloging-in-Publication Data

ISBN 978-1-62081-276-1

Published by Nova Science Publishers, Inc. † New York

CONTENTS

PREFACE

Although Turkey still depends on the United States and other NATO allies for political and strategic support, growing economic diversification and military self-reliance allows Turkey to exercise greater leverage with the West. These trends have helped fuel continuing Turkish political transformation led in the past decade by Prime Minister Recep Tayyip Erdogan and the Justice and Development Party (AKP), which has Islamist roots. Future domestic political developments may determine how Turkey reconciles respect for democratic views that favor Turkish nationalism and traditional Sunni Muslim values with protection of individual freedoms, minority rights, rule of law, and the principle of secular governance. This book examines U.S. relations with Turkey, with a focus on domestic and foreign policy issues; the decline in Israel-Turkey relations; and ongoing change in the Middle East region.

Chapter 1- Congress has an active role to play in shaping and overseeing U.S. relations with Turkey, and several Turkish domestic and foreign policy issues have significant relevance for U.S. interests. This chapter provides background information on Turkey and discusses possible policy options for Members of Congress and the Obama Administration. U.S. relations with Turkey—a longtime North Atlantic Treaty Organization (NATO) ally—have evolved over time as global challenges to U.S. interests have changed. Turkey's economic dynamism and geopolitical importance—it straddles Europe, the Middle East, and Central Asia and now has the world's 16th-largest economy—have increased its influence regionally and globally. Although Turkey still depends on the United States and other NATO allies for political and strategic support, growing economic diversification and military self-reliance allows Turkey to exercise greater leverage with the West. These trends have helped fuel continuing Turkish political transformation led in the past decade by Prime Minister Recep Tayyip Erdogan and the Justice and Development Party (AKP), which has Islamist roots. Future domestic political developments may determine how Turkey reconciles respect for democratic views that favor Turkish nationalism and traditional Sunni Muslim values with protection of individual freedoms, minority rights, rule of law, and the principle of secular governance. Debate on issues such as the status of Turkey's ethnic Kurdish population, the civil-military balance, the role of religion in public life, and heightened concern over press freedom could coalesce in 2012 around a proposal for a new constitution. Congressional interest in Turkey is high with respect to the following issues:

Chapter 2- Congress and the Obama Administration are seeking to manage longstanding bilateral and North Atlantic Treaty Organization (NATO)-based defense cooperation with Turkey at a time when a more independent Turkish foreign policy course and changes in regional security conditions are creating new challenges for both countries. Defense cooperation rooted in shared threat perceptions from the Cold War era and built on close U.S. ties with the Turkish military leadership now must be reconciled with a decline of the military's political influence in Turkish society and some negative turns in Turkish popular sentiment toward the United States over the past decade. At the same time, Turkey's importance as a U.S. ally has arguably increased on issues of global significance in its surrounding region that include Iraq, Iran, Afghanistan, and the Israeli-Palestinian peace process. In early 2011, Turkey's regional role has arguably become even more prominent—exemplified by its significant involvement politically and militarily on the question of NATO's intervention in Libya.

Chapter 3- Israel unilaterally withdrew from the Gaza Strip in 2005, but retained control of its borders. Hamas, a U.S. State Department-designated Foreign Terrorist Organization (FTO), won the 2006 Palestinian legislative elections and forcibly seized control of the territory in 2007. Israel imposed a tighter blockade of Gaza in response to Hamas's takeover and tightened the flow of goods and materials into Gaza after its military offensive against Hamas from December 2008 to January 2009. That offensive destroyed much of Gaza's infrastructure, but Israel has obstructed the delivery of rebuilding materials that it said could also be used to manufacture weapons and for other military purposes. Israel, the U.N., and international non-governmental organizations differ about the severity of the blockade's effects on the humanitarian situation of Palestinian residents of Gaza. Nonetheless, it is clear that the territory's economy and people are suffering.

In: Turkey and the U.S.
Editors: S. N. Boothe and R. Hickman
ISBN: 978-1- 62081-276-1

Chapter 1

TURKEY: BACKGROUND AND UNITED STATES RELATIONS*

Jim Zanotti

SUMMARY

Congress has an active role to play in shaping and overseeing U.S. relations with Turkey, and several Turkish domestic and foreign policy issues have significant relevance for U.S. interests. This report provides background information on Turkey and discusses possible policy options for Members of Congress and the Obama Administration. U.S. relations with Turkey—a longtime North Atlantic Treaty Organization (NATO) ally—have evolved over time as global challenges to U.S. interests have changed. Turkey's economic dynamism and geopolitical importance—it straddles Europe, the Middle East, and Central Asia and now has the world's 16th-largest economy—have increased its influence regionally and globally. Although Turkey still depends on the United States and other NATO allies for political and strategic support, growing economic diversification and military self-reliance allows Turkey to exercise greater leverage with the West. These trends have helped fuel continuing Turkish political transformation led in the past decade by Prime Minister Recep Tayyip Erdogan and the Justice and Development Party (AKP), which has Islamist roots. Future domestic political developments may determine

* This is an edited, reformatted and augmented version of Congressional Research Service, Publication No. R41368, dated January 24, 2012.

how Turkey reconciles respect for democratic views that favor Turkish nationalism and traditional Sunni Muslim values with protection of individual freedoms, minority rights, rule of law, and the principle of secular governance. Debate on issues such as the status of Turkey's ethnic Kurdish population, the civil-military balance, the role of religion in public life, and heightened concern over press freedom could coalesce in 2012 around a proposal for a new constitution. Congressional interest in Turkey is high with respect to the following issues:

- Addressing ongoing change in the Middle East by coordinating policies and using Turkey's regional example to influence political outcomes in Syria, Iraq, Afghanistan, and elsewhere; counter Iranian influence; and preserve stability;
- The decline in Israel-Turkey relations and how that might affect U.S.-Turkey defense cooperation, including arms sales to counter the Kurdistan Workers' Party (PKK), a U.S.-designated Foreign Terrorist Organization; and
- A potential congressional resolution or presidential statement on the possible genocide of Armenians by the Ottoman Empire (Turkey's predecessor state) during World War I.

Many U.S. policymakers also are interested in the rights of minority Christian communities within Turkey; the currently stalemated prospects of Turkish accession to the European Union (EU); promoting increased trade with Turkey; and Turkey's role in the Cyprus dispute, especially given tensions in late 2011 over offshore gas drilling in the Eastern Mediterranean. Congress annually appropriates less than $10 million in military and security assistance for Turkey. The EU currently provides over $1 billion to Turkey annually in pre-accession financial and technical assistance. In 2011, U.S.-Turkey cooperation on issues affecting the Middle East became closer, partly because Turkey agreed to host a U.S. radar as part of a NATO missile defense system. Nevertheless, developments during the Obama Administration—including Erdogan's downgrading of relations with Israel—have led to questions about the extent to which U.S. and Turkish strategic priorities and values converge on both a short- and long-term basis. Issues on which congressional action could affect future cooperation one way or another include the possible sale of drone aircraft to Turkey to counter the PKK and a potential Armenian genocide resolution.

INTRODUCTION AND ISSUES FOR CONGRESS

Turkey has been an important ally for the United States since the Cold War era. As global challenges to U.S. interests have changed over time, U.S. relations with Turkey have evolved. During that time, Turkey has experienced fundamental internal change—particularly the economic empowerment of a middle class from its Anatolian heartland that emphasizes traditional Sunni Muslim values. This change has helped fuel continuing political transformation led in the past decade by Prime Minister Recep Tayyip Erdogan, President Abdullah Gul, and Foreign Minister Ahmet Davutoglu (all of whom are profiled in Appendix A) from the Islamic-leaning Justice and Development Party (known by its Turkish acronym, AKP, or *Adalet ve Kalkinma Partisi*). For decades, the Turkish republic relied upon its military, judiciary, and other bastions of its "secular elite" to protect it from political and ideological extremes—sacrificing at least some of its democratic vitality in the process. Through a series of elections, popular referenda, court decisions and other political developments within the existing constitutional order, Turkey has changed into a more civilian-led system that increasingly reflects the new middle class's dedication to market economics and conservative values.

Turkey's internal transformation has at least partly driven increased engagement and influence within its own region and the Muslim world, where its leaders have aspired to a foreign policy of "zero problems." At the same time, its leaders have tried to maintain Turkey's traditional alliances and economic partnerships with Western nations in the North Atlantic Treaty Organization (NATO) and the European Union (EU), routinely asserting that Turkey's location at the crossroads of Europe and Asia and its increasing soft power provides it and its allies with "strategic depth." Thus, the geopolitical importance of Turkey for the United States in a post-September 11, 2011, world is now intertwined with its importance as a regional partner and symbol—politically, culturally, economically, and religiously.

Congressional interest in Turkey is high with respect to the following issues and questions:

- *Addressing Regional Change in the Greater Middle East*: Will Turkey's policies and actions be reconcilable with U.S. interests in countries such as Syria, Iraq, Egypt, Tunisia, Libya, and Afghanistan with regard to political and financial support for populations, opposetion movements, and transitional governments; existing and potential future sanctions against autocratic regimes; internationally mandated humanitarian and/or military action that includes or may include the use of Turkish bases or territory; and limiting Iranian influence?

- *Israel and U.S.-Turkey Defense Cooperation*: Will increasing tensions in Turkey-Israel relations hamper U.S. efforts at regional security coordination? Should these tensions affect congressional views generally on Turkey's status as a U.S. ally and/or specifically on sales of weapons—particularly those such as drone aircraft that involve highly sensitive technology—that Turkey seeks to combat the Kurdistan Workers' Party (PKK, or *Partiya Karkaren Kurdistan*), a U.S.-designated Foreign Terrorist Organization?
- *Armenian Genocide Resolution*: What are the arguments for and against a potential U.S. congressional resolution or presidential statement characterizing World War I-era deaths of hundreds of thousands of Armenians through actions of Ottoman Empire (Turkey's predecessor state) authorities as genocide, including considerations of how such a resolution would affect U.S.-Turkey relations and defense cooperation?
- *Rights of Non-Muslim Minority Religions*: What is Congress's proper role in promoting the rights of established Christian and Jewish communities and religious leaderships and their associated foundations within Turkey to choose leaders, train clergy, own property, and otherwise function independent of the Turkish government?

As of January 2012, there are 131 Members of Congress in the Congressional Caucus on Turkey and Turkish Americans.[1] Congress appro-priates relatively small amounts of military and security assistance for Turkey compared with past sums—approximately $8 million in FY2011, with less than $6 million requested by the Obama Administration for FY2012. The Administration does not currently request, nor does Congress appropriate, Economic Support Fund assistance for Turkey—perhaps partly owing to the over $1 billion in pre-accession financial and technical assistance Turkey receives from the European Union (EU).

Many U.S. policymakers also are interested in the currently stalemated prospects of Turkish accession to the EU; promoting increased trade with Turkey; and Turkey's role in the Cyprus dispute, especially given tensions in late 2011 over offshore gas drilling in the Eastern Mediterranean. Domestic Turkish political developments, possibly including a new constitution in 2012, seem likely to affect the country's civil-military balance, its debate on religion in public life, the status of its Kurdish and other minorities, and heightened concerns about press and civil society freedoms, which are in turn likely to determine who shapes Turkey's foreign policy and how they conduct it. Turkey's continued regional influence could depend on its maintaining the robust economic growth from its past decade that has led to its having the world's 16th-largest economy. Gauging how U.S. and Turkish interests coincide has become increasingly complicated and dynamic. In 2011, U.S.-Turkish closeness on issues affecting the Middle East increased because

- Turkish leaders perceive a need for U.S. help to encourage regional democratic transition while countering actors with the potential to undermine internal Turkish and regional stability—including the Iranian and Syrian regimes and terrorists from its own ethnic Kurdish population; and
- The United States may be more dependent on its alliance with Turkey because the end of its military mission in Iraq and other possible future reductions in its Middle East footprint probably give Turkey greater influence over developments in Iraq and other parts of the region whose stability is of critical U.S. interest.

These factors have led to frequent high-level U.S.-Turkey consultation on developments in Syria, Libya, and the broader region. In addition, U.S. officials reportedly interpreted Turkey's agreement in September 2011 to host a U.S. early warning radar as part of a NATO missile defense system for Europe as a critical sign of Turkey's interest in continued strategic cooperation with Washington.[4] During the previous year, some U.S. and European policymakers and analysts had voiced concern about Turkey's reliability as a bilateral and NATO ally owing to its active opposition to United Nations sanctions against Iran for its nuclear program and its deteriorating relationship with and criticism of Israel—particularly in the wake of the May 2010 Gaza flotilla incident that resulted in the death of eight Turks and an American of Turkish origin.

Short-term fluctuations in the U.S.-Turkey relationship could become the norm as greater fluidity in domestic, regional, and global developments leads both actors to more frequently reassess their circumstances and positions vis-à-vis each other and significant third party actors. The two countries' acceptance of this situation might lead to shared longer-term views regarding mutual interests that facilitate broad strategic cooperation, or to more limited expectations regarding the conditions and timing under which they might make common cause.

Table 1. Turkey in Brief

Population:	78,785,548 (July 2011 est.)
Area:	783,562 sq km (302,535 sq. mi., slightly larger than Texas)
Most Populous Cities:	Istanbul 11.2 mil., Ankara 4.1 mil., Izmir 3.2 mil., Bursa 2.0 mil., Adana 1.6 mil. (2007 est.
Ethnic Groups:	Turks 70%-75%; Kurds 18%; Other minorities 7%-12% (2008 est.)
Religion:	Muslim 99.8% (Sunni 75%-88%, Alevi 12%-25%), Others (mainly Christian and Jewish) 0.2%
Literacy:	87% (male 95%, female 80%) (2004 est.)2
% of Population 14 or Younger:	26.6% (2011 est.)3
GDP Per Capita:	$10,624 (2011 est.)
Real GDP Growth:	7.5% (2011 est.)
Inflation:	6.2% (2011 est.)
Unemployment:	8.8% (2011 est.)
External Debt as % of GDP:	43% (2011 est.)
Current Account	
(Trade) Deficit as % of GDP:	9.8% (2011 est.)

Sources: Turkish Ministry of Economy, OECD Economic Outlook, Economist Intelligence Unit, Central Intelligence Agency World Factbook, Turkish Statistics Institute.

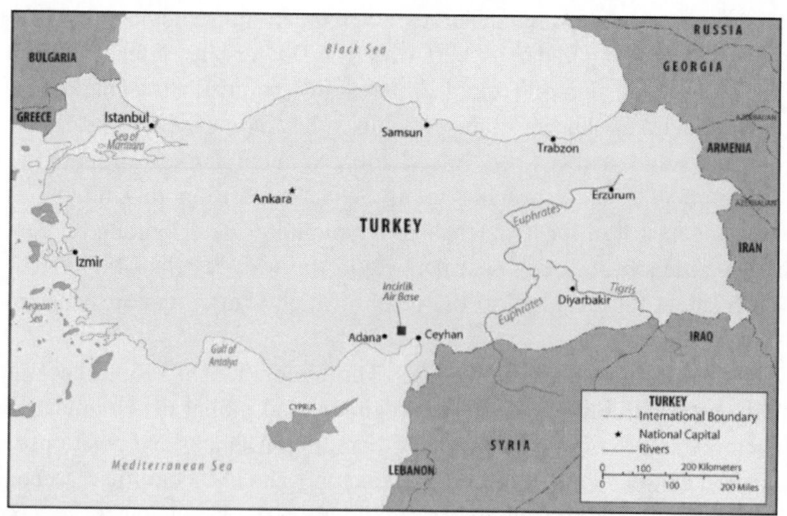

Source: CRS Graphics.

Figure 1. Turkey and Its Neighbors.

Background and Domestic Political Issues

Since the end of the Cold War in the early 1990s, a number of developments have transformed Turkey and its relationship with the United States. Per capita income has more than tripled (from approximately $3,000 to over $10,000) in the past decade. Economic dynamism and Turkey's geopolitical importance—straddling Europe, the Middle East, and Central Asia—have increased its influence regionally and globally. Although Turkey still depends on the United States and other NATO allies for political and strategic support, growing economic diversification and military ties with non-NATO countries have contributed to greater Turkish leverage with the West. A number of internal and external developments have contributed to political changes, most notably the rise of the AKP and the dwindling capacity of the military and other bulwarks of Turkey's traditional secular elite to counter the initiatives of elected government representatives. Over the past decade, Prime Minister Erdogan has consolidated the AKP's hold on power.

Historical Overview

Starting with the founding of the Turkish Republic in 1923 by Mustafa Kemal Ataturk, state officials self-consciously sought to define Turkey as a secular state patterning itself after the West politically, legally, socially, economically, and militarily. The military was the ultimate protector of a Kemalist order that included state control of religion; discontinuing the use of Arabic script in favor of the Latin alphabet; discouraging Islamic modes of dress; and actively promoting literacy, education, and employment among men and women of all classes and backgrounds.

Changes to the Kemalist Order

In the Past Decade

That the old order is changing is clearly manifested by the political mandate enjoyed for the past decade by the AKP, which has Islamist roots. These changes have gained greater attention and momentum through failed attempts (or purported attempts) by elements within the military, the judiciary, the opposition Republican People's Party (known by its Turkish acronym, CHP, or *Cumhuriyet Halk Partisi*), and others within the Turkish secular elite to thwart the AKP on key issues. Major AKP victories in the face of domestic pressure included:

- the 2007 election within parliament of the AKP's Abdullah Gul (a former prime minister and foreign minister) as Turkey's president;
- alleged unsuccessful plots to undermine or overthrow the government;
- the unsuccessful 2008 Constitutional Court case attempting to ban and dissolve the AKP; and
- the September 2010 passage of amendments to the 1982 military-backed constitution in a nationwide referendum, increasing military and judicial accountability to civilian and democratic institutions.[5]

Additionally, in July 2011, on the eve of the annual Turkish Supreme Military Council meetings to discuss promotions and retirements, the chief of the Turkish General Staff (TGS), Isik Kosaner, resigned simultaneously with the generals who commanded the Turkish land, naval, and air forces. According to most reports and Kosaner's account, the resignations were connected with the generals' concern about the government's detention or passing over of several high-ranking officers. Civilian leaders opposed rewarding officers allegedly involved in plots purportedly hatched within the military in the early 2000s (called "Ergenekon" and "Sledgehammer") to overthrow or undermine the AKP government. Many analysts have portrayed Kosaner's resignation and his subsequent replacement by Necdet Ozel, previously the commander of the Turkish Gendarmerie, as an indication that domestic power has shifted decisively to civilian government leaders, who are now able to appoint more deferential and constrained military leaders.[6] In January 2012, Turkish authorities took the unprecedented step of arresting former TGS Chief Ilker Basbug in connection with the Ergenekon case. One Turkish analyst was quoted as saying in reaction, "The fact that prosecutors are now touching senior generals is a turning point in the democratization process of Turkey."[7]

In Historical and Societal Context

The changes to the old order did not materialize suddenly with the AKP's rise to power. They reflect long-standing dynamics in Turkish politics and society that continue to evolve within Turkey's existing constitutional framework. Popular desires to allow greater public space for traditional Islamic-oriented lifestyles and societal participation manifested themselves politically as early as the 1950s during the rule of Turkey's first democratically elected leader, Adnan Menderes. Menderes was eventually overthrown by a military-led coup in 1960 (and subsequently hanged), and the military continued to discourage the overt influence of religion in politics, intervening again in 1971 and 1980 to replace governments that it deemed had lost control of the country or had steered it away from secularism or toward ideological extremes.

The military allowed Deputy Prime Minister for Economic Affairs (later Prime Minister and President) Turgut Ozal to begin liberalizing the traditionally statist Turkish economy following its restoration of internal order in 1980. This helped set in motion a chain of events leading to the economic and political empowerment of millions of Turks hailing from traditional communities removed from Turkey's more secular urban centers. Subsequent social and political developments reflected accommodation of this rising middle class—many of whom migrated to bigger cities— and their values. For example, *imam hatip* religious schools, initially established for young males seeking clerical careers, became widely attended by youth from religiously conservative families.[8] In 1997, Turkey's first-ever Islamist-led coalition government was compelled to resign by the military, but junior members of the coalition-leading Refah (Welfare) Party went on to form the AKP,[9] which they characterize as a center-right reformist party without an Islamist agenda.

Popular discontent with coalition rule stemming from a 1999-2001 economic and financial crisis and perceptions of government corruption and ineffectiveness opened the way for the AKP to achieve single-party rule with its first election victory in 2002. Since the AKP came to power, the military has reportedly become less scrutinizing of its rising officers' religious backgrounds and views, taxes and regulations on the consumption of alcohol have increased, and the wearing of headscarves by women in universities and other public places has gained legal and social acceptance.

Domestic and international observers have raised concerns about the AKP government's respect for civil liberties.[10] Although infringement upon press freedom is of routine concern in Turkey, recent measures taken by authorities have been criticized inside and outside of Turkey as unusually severe and ideologically driven.[11] These measures include multiple arrests of journalists and multi-billion-dollar tax fraud penalties against the country's largest pro-secularist media firm (the Dogan Group).[12]

Concerns about press freedom exist against the backdrop of ongoing criminal investigations into the Ergenekon and Sledgehammer cases discussed above. Many in the media claim that even if some of the anti-government plots were real, authorities with pro-AKP leanings or sympathies for the Fethullah Gulen movement (discussed below) have used the allegations to silence or weaken political and ideological opponents.[13] Concerns about AKP overreach reflect anxieties among some Turks that, with the weakening of the military and other guardians of the Kemalist order, it is unclear to what extent effective checks and balances exist on Erdogan's charismatic and Islamic-friendly single-party rule.

Fethullah Gulen Movement

The Fethullah Gulen movement (or community) became a nationwide grassroots movement in the 1980s as part of the emergence of the new conservative Turkish middle class. Its societal rise has roughly paralleled the AKP's political rise, and Gulen-inspired businesses, media enterprises, and civil society organizations now exercise considerable influence in Turkey.[14] The movement is comprised of adherents of Turkish imam Fethullah Gulen, who is now a permanent U.S. resident,[15] and who insists that he is neutral as to political parties and leaders in Turkey.[16] Gulen preaches a distinctly Turkish brand of Islam that condemns terrorism[17] and can function in concert with secular democratic mechanisms and modern economic and technological modes of living. Gulenist-affiliated organizations also maintain a presence in the United States[18] and other regions worldwide.

The parallel rise of the AKP and the Gulen movement has unsettled many pro-secularist Turks who detect greater ideological bias within Turkish state and civil society institutions and who are concerned about the potential for imposition of Islamic norms and suppression of dissent. Other observers see the AKP's and Gulenists' emergence as an authentic and even necessary development in Turkey's democratic evolution because of their views' representativeness of large segments of the population. This, in these observers' view, provides a counterbalance to Turkish secularist ideology that in the past had been rigidly enforced and inculcated.

Economy and Trade

The AKP's political successes have been aided considerably by robust Turkish economic growth that was set back only briefly as a result of the 2008-2009 global economic crisis. Growth rates, fueled by diversified Turkish conglomerates such as Sabanci and Koc as well as "Anatolian tigers" (small- to medium-sized, export-oriented businesses concentrated in central and southern Turkey), have been comparable in the past decade to those of China, India, and other major developing economies. According to the Turkish

Ministry of Economy, Turkey's construction industry, with extensive projects domestically as well as in Russia, Central Asia, the Balkans, the Middle East, and Africa, was listed by *Engineering News Record* in 2010 as second only to China's in the number of projects undertaken worldwide.[19] Its dependence on foreign investment and exports could bring on future challenges from a potential economic slowdown in the European Union—Turkey's main trading partner.

An Organization for Economic Cooperation and Development (OECD) forecast from 2009 projected that Turkey's economy would grow at the highest rate of any OECD member from 2011 to 2017, with projected average annual real GDP growth of 6.7%.[20] However, a potential Europe-related slowdown could slow 2012 growth to between 2% and 4%. Recent monetary policy decisions by Turkey's central bank to lower interest rates have limited foreign capital inflows and contributed to current consumer-spending-driven growth. They also have contributed to a depreciation in Turkey's currency (the lira) that might help Turkey with its import-export balance, but also possibly fuel inflation,[21] which Turkey seeks to control through relatively conservative fiscal policies and banking practices. Major Turkish exports include textiles, foodstuffs, iron and steel, and machinery; while major imports include chemicals, fuels, and semi-finished goods. Structural economic goals for Turkey include incentivizing greater research and development to encourage Turkish technological innovation and global competitiveness, harmonizing the educational system with future workforce needs, and increasing and diversifying energy supplies to meet ever-growing consumption demands.

The European Union is Turkey's main trading partner by far, while the United States is Turkey's fourth-largest trading partner (behind the EU, Russia, and China—see "Bilateral Trade Promotion" below). Though Turkish pursuit of new markets since 1991 has reduced trade with both the EU (from nearly 50% to just over 40%) and the United States (from over 9% to under 5%) as a percentage of Turkey's total trade, overall trade volume with both continues to increase. Over the same period, trade with Russia as a percentage of Turkey's total trade has more than doubled—from 5% to over 11%—largely due to energy imports. China's share of Turkish trade is also increasing, with volume reportedly rising from $1 billion per year to $24 billion per year in the past decade.[22] Iran (as discussed below) is—like Russia—a major source of Turkish energy. Turkey's importance as a regional energy transport corridor (see "Turkey as a Transit Corridor and Potential Source" below) elevates Turkey's increasing relevance for world energy markets while also providing Turkey with opportunities to satisfy its own growing domestic energy needs.[23] Additionally, Turkey has actively pursued economic opportunities with many Arab Middle Eastern countries in recent years through free trade and no-visa agreements. As political upheaval in the region continues, it could contribute to future challenges to Turkish economic growth and foreign investment.

Major Minority Groups

Kurds

Ethnic Kurds constitute 15%-20% of Turkey's population, and are concentrated in urban areas and the relatively impoverished southeastern region of the country. Kurdish reluctance to recognize Turkish state authority—a dynamic that also exists between Kurds and national governments in Iraq, Iran, and Syria—and harsh Turkish measures to quell claims of Kurdish identity have fed tensions that have periodically worsened since the foundation of the republic in 1923. Since 1984, the Turkish military has waged an off-and-on struggle to put down a separatist insurgency and urban terrorism campaign by the PKK (whose founder, Abdullah Ocalan, is profiled in Appendix A).[24] This struggle was most intense during the 1990s, but resumed after a lull in 2003 after the U.S.-led invasion of Iraq. The PKK uses safe havens in northern Iraq to coordinate and launch attacks, and according to the U.S. government partially finances its activities through criminal activities, including its operation of a Europe-wide drug trafficking network.[25] The initially secessionist demands of the PKK have since evolved to a less ambitious goal of greater cultural and political autonomy. The Turkish military's approach to neutralizing the PKK has been routinely criticized by Western governments and human rights organizations for being overly hard on ethnic Kurds—thousands have been imprisoned for PKK involvement or sympathies and hundreds of thousands have been displaced.

Turkey's AKP government—which has a sizeable constituency in rural Kurdish areas because of its appeal to traditional values—has acknowledged that the integration of Kurds into Turkish society will require political, cultural, and economic development approaches in addition to the more traditional security-based approach. By appealing to common Islamic identity, Erdogan and other government ministers have moved away from the state's traditional unwillingness to acknowledge the multiethnic nature of Turkey's citizenry. Thus far, however, government statements or efforts aimed at giving greater rights to Kurds and greater normalized status to Kurdish nationalist leaders and former militants have been politically undermined by upswings in PKK attacks and public manifestations of Kurdish nationalist pride. The government has adopted some measures allowing greater use of Kurdish languages in education, election campaigns, and the media. Kurdish nationalist leaders demand that any future changes to Turkey's constitution not suppress Kurdish ethnic and linguistic identity. They also seek to modify the electoral law to allow for greater Kurdish nationalist participation in Turkish politics by lowering the percentage-vote threshold (currently 10%) for political parties in parliament.[26]

Alevis

Most Muslims in Turkey are Sunni, but 10 million to 20 million are Alevis (of whom about 20% are ethnic Kurds). The Alevi sect of Islam is an offshoot of Shiism[27] that contains strands from pre-Islamic Anatolian traditions. Alevism has been traditionally influenced by Sufi mysticism that emphasizes believers' individual spiritual paths, but it defies precise description owing to its lack of centralized leadership and reliance on oral traditions historically kept secret from outsiders. Alevis have long been among the strongest supporters of Turkey's secular state, which they perceive as their protector from the Sunni majority.

A New Constitution?

The AKP has proposed that a new constitution replace the one imposed by the military in 1982. Most observers expect that a new constitution would more firmly place the state's governing mechanisms—including the executive, military, judiciary, Supreme Electoral Council, Council of Higher Education, and Supreme Board of Radio and Television—under democratic civilian control.

Other possible changes include greater emphasis on individual rights and greater delegation of authority to provincial and local officials. It is unclear whether furthering civilian control in an era of AKP dominance is compatible with the goal of strengthening Turkish civil liberties and decentralizing state power.

Future debate over a new constitution and its implementation might include discussion of the potential merits and drawbacks of single-party rule and robust executive power. Do Turks prefer a system that is more subject to the personal direction of popular leaders, or one that might sacrifice some expediency of action in favor of greater consensus across party and ideological lines? This debate could be shaped by Turkey's economic outlook and its citizens' concerns about potential national security threats.

Although the AKP's June 2011 electoral victory provided it with a significant mandate and nearly 50% of the vote, its inability to garner a 60% supermajority in Turkey's unicameral parliament (the Turkish Grand National Assembly) has led most analysts to conclude that the AKP will need to find opposition support for its constitutional proposals.

The need for consensus has dimmed the prospect that Erdogan could use the constitutional reform process to vest greater power in the presidency—an office that he may seek near the end of his current term as prime minister.

A Constitutional Reconciliation Commission including all four parties represented in parliament—the AKP, the secular-leaning CHP, the Nationalist Action Party (MHP), and the Kurdish nationalist Peace and Democracy Party (BDP)—was formed in late 2011, led by Parliamentary Speaker Cemil Cicek, who has stated his goal of having a new constitution approved by popular referendum by the end of 2012.

Analysts debate whether Erdogan will seek to redefine himself as a more consensus-oriented politician in the debate over constitutional reform, or whether he will try to establish his preferences by applying greater political pressure on his opponents if significant disagreements arise.

Table 2. Parties in Turkey's Parliament
(Based on national elections held in June 2011)

Party	June 2011 Pct Vote	Members of Parliament	General Orientation
Justice and Development Party (AKP) Leader: Recep Tayyip Erdogan	49.8%	326	Economic liberalism, social conservatism
Republican People's Party (CHP) Leader: Kemal Kilicdaroglu	26.0%	135	Social democracy, pro-secular
Nationalist Action Party (MHP) Leader: Devlet Bahceli	13.0%	53	Nationalism
Peace and Democracy Party (BDP) Leader: Selahattin Demirtas	6.6%a	36	Ethnic Kurdish interests, social democracy

Source: Supreme Electoral Board of Turkey, Parties and Elections in Europe Website.

[a] This is the percentage vote figure for the 61 BDP members who ran in the election as independents for individual geographic constituencies, as described in footnote 26.

BDP support for constitutional proposals that address the questions of Kurdish civil, linguistic, and cultural rights and local autonomy could become particularly important in light of increases in PKK violence and Turkish reprisals following the June election, as discussed above. The first clause of Article 3 of the 1982 constitution reads, "The Turkish state, with its territory and nation, is an indivisible entity. Its language is Turkish." Because the constitution states that its first three articles are unamendable, even proposing a change could face judicial obstacles. Some observers believe that recent arrests of prominent BDP members and other Kurdish nationalist political activists, as well as a December 2011 Turkish air strike that mistakenly killed 35 civilians,[28] might be souring the atmosphere for constitutional compromise.

The AKP government maintains that a new constitution will advance democratization and help the country meet criteria for EU membership. In one European observer's analysis of constitutional changes, however, "European integration and democratization [in Turkey] are increasingly hostage to the struggle for power among the elites": the "not-so-new" AKP ruling elite and the "remnants of the so-called Kemalist establishment."[29]

Minority Religious Rights

While U.S. constitutional law prohibits the excessive entanglement of the government with religion, republican Turkey has maintained secularism by controlling or closely overseeing religious activities in the country—partly in order to counter the openly Islamic nature of previous centuries of Ottoman rule. Sunni Muslims, although not monolithic in their views on freedom of worship, have better recourse than other religious adherents to the democratic process for accommodation of their views because of their majority status. Minority Muslim sects (most prominently, the Alevis) and non-Muslim religions largely depend on legal appeals, political advocacy, and outside support from Western countries to protect their rights in Turkey.

U.S. and congressional concerns focus on the rights of established Christian and Jewish communities and religious leaderships and their associated foundations and organizations within Turkey to choose leaders, train clergy, own property, and otherwise function independently of the Turkish government.[30] Grievances are routinely expressed by Members of Congress through proposed congressional resolutions and through letters to the President and to Turkish leaders on behalf of the Ecumenical Patriarchate of Constantinople, the spiritual center of Orthodox Christianity based in Istanbul.[31] On

December 13, 2011, for example, the House passed H.Res. 306—"Urging the Republic of Turkey to safeguard its Christian heritage and to return confiscated church properties"—by voice vote.[32]

During the early years of the Turkish Republic, the state began confiscating the properties of religious groups as part of its efforts to control religious life in the country. In late August 2011, Prime Minister Erdogan announced that Turkey would return properties confiscated since the adoption of a 1936 law governing religious foundations, to the extent the properties are still held publicly.[33] Properties to be returned potentially include schools, orphanages, cemeteries, commercial properties, and hospitals affiliated with various Orthodox and Catholic churches and Turkey's Jewish community. According to one report, "The government's willingness to explore restitution does not yet cover the hundreds, if not thousands, of property seizures from individuals, or the takeovers that occurred before 1936. An even more contentious point is confiscation that occurred prior to the formation of the Republic of Turkey in 1923."[34] According to a U.S. diplomat based in Turkey, a Greek school in Istanbul was returned to a religious community association in November 2011, with more property returns expected in the near future pursuant to each organization's application for return of applicable properties and the determination of the government's General Directorate of Foundations.[35] Prior to this decree, the European Court of Human Rights made multiple rulings requiring Turkey to pay compensation to various religious-affiliated organizations after earlier attempts by the government to remedy the situation did not satisfy the organizations.

FOREIGN POLICY ON MATTERS OF U.S. INTEREST

The "Turkish Model" and Regional Stance

As unrest and political change have occurred across much of the Arab Middle East since late 2010, Turkey might perceive that the United States has greater need of Turkish support in the region. Turkey exercises considerable regional influence given its military, economic, and political power—aided by its status as an established Muslim-majority democracy and its membership in NATO.

Political activists in several countries facing leadership transitions or potential transitions— including Tunisia and Egypt—have cited Turkey as a potential model for their own political systems. This has raised questions among leaders and analysts about which aspects of Turkey's system these activists seek to emulate—whether it is its outwardly secular mechanisms, its historical military guardianship, its economic vitality, its political system in which civilian leaders with Islamist leanings have exerted increasing power, or some combination of these.

Arab interpretations of the "Turkish model" tend to emphasize the recent democratic and economic empowerment of Turkey's middle class and the connection between this and Turkey's emergence as a regional power with a foreign policy independent of the West. Some Western views favor some notion of military guardianship of the state from disorder and ideological extremes (a model that many Westerners have historically equated with republican Turkey).[36] While some in both the Arab world and the West suspect that Turkey's government favors the rise of pro-democracy Islamist movements that emulate the AKP, Prime Minister Erdogan was criticized by North African Islamists during his September 2011 trip to Egypt, Tunisia, and Libya for voicing his support for secular democratic mechanisms. Many analysts and Turkish officials have stated that Turkey might more aptly be characterized as an inspiration than as a model because the historical experiences and characteristics of its people, society, and economic system are distinct from those in Arab countries.[37]

Within the context of ongoing regional change, Turkey has sought to balance its support for country-specific democratic reforms with its interests in overall stability. Turkish interests appear to be threefold: (1) It is the leading Muslim-majority democracy in the region with an interest in promoting its political values, (2) it has a significant economic stake in the region, and (3) it is concerned about the regional balance of power and possible spillover effects for its own security. Turkish leaders are particularly concerned about developments at or near its borders with Syria and Iraq, especially given Turkey's own on-and-off struggles with Kurdish separatist militants who maintain safe havens in northern Iraq and who could be further strengthened by their fellow ethnic Kurds in Syria, Iraq, and Iran if those states' governments are weakened.

In 2011-2012, Turkey has shown greater openness to supporting U.S. and NATO goals in the region than it did prior to the widespread political change. One could argue that in the wake of the Iraq war, Turkey believed that U.S. intervention in the region had played a large part in creating or exacerbating political instabilities and sectarian tensions that fueled regional security threats, including the terrorist threat Turkey faces from the PKK. Some analysts postulated that Turkey's opposition to U.N. sanctions against Iran and greater closeness with Iran, Syria, and Hamas were based on a belief in the superiority of a regional security order with more local and less U.S. and Western involvement.

The changes of 2011 appear to have altered Turkey's stance on this question. One of Turkey's concerns is that region-wide unrest, especially in neighboring Syria, could endanger the political stability of the entire area and possibly jeopardize Turkey's political and economic influence in the region. Turkish leaders also may have concluded that U.S. involvement—while perhaps not without risks—is desirable on balance in order to counter Iranian and possibly Syrian capacities and designs for capitalizing on regional uncertainty. This could at least partly account for Turkey's agreement in September 2011 to host the missile defense radar discussed above, which is generally thought to be focused on defending against potential Iranian missile threats to Europe. After Turkish leaders were unable to use their supposedly close relations with the Asad regime in Syria and the Qadhafi regime in Libya to persuade either regime to address demands of protesting citizens and opposition groups, they accepted and to some extent adopted the U.S. and European approach of supporting opposition groups and sanctions against those regimes.

This change in approach by Prime Minister Erdogan seems consistent with his desire to project a regionally populist stance that is not viewed by Arab populations as siding with autocrats or entrenched commercial interests. Turkey may seek even greater U.S. help to maintain regional stability if unfolding events significantly disrupt its security or threaten Turkish trade or attraction of outside investment.

However, as one Turkish analyst has written, interpreting Turkey's changes in regional policy as signaling a fundamental shift toward greater closeness to the West may be overstating matters in the same way that Turkey's supposed shift away from the West may have been overstated in earlier years:

> Turkey's behavior is driven by the same objective as ever. Partnership with the West, at this current juncture, is a valuable instrument as long as it enhances Ankara's ability to meet the new challenges and expands the room to maneuver, not because of its inherent value. The quest for strategic autonomy still instructs Turkish leaders' thinking on international affairs, and is unlikely to disappear.[38]

Several observers noted in late 2011 that Turkey's aspirations for a zero-problem foreign policy at its borders may be at an end given reversals in its relations with Syria and Iran. In this regard, two analysts from the International Crisis Group asserted that

> Turkey may be left with a foreign policy with no conceptual framework to unite its many contradictions: an unsustainable mix of alliance with the U.S. and confrontation with Israel; a social-economic model built on convergence with Europe but in which the EU negotiation process has stalled; idealistic enthusiasm for Muslim democrats but continued links to other authoritarian leaders; public displays of Muslim piety alongside support for secular constitutions; and bitter arguments with all those keen to capitalize on the above to cast doubt on Turkey's role in the Middle East.[39]

Israel

In the 1990s and early 2000s, Turkey and Israel enjoyed close military ties that fostered and reinforced cooperation in other areas, including a free trade agreement signed in 2000. In recent years, however, Turkey-Israel relations have worsened. This downturn can be attributed to a number of factors, including the May 2010 Gaza flotilla incident (mentioned above) and Turkish-Israeli differences over Israel's invasion of Hamas-controlled Gaza in December 2008. It also parallels the military's declining role in Turkish society, and the greater empowerment of Prime Minister Erdogan and other AKP and national leaders who seem increasingly to believe that criticizing many of Israel's policies is both merited and domestically popular.

Turkey's deteriorated relationship with Israel, which Erdogan may be emphasizing to some extent as part of his strategy to gather populist regional support, presents problems for the United States because of the U.S. desire to coordinate its regional policies with two of its closest allies. Although a lack of rapprochement may not render U.S. security coordination efforts impossible, it could have eventual repercussions for regional order and undermine the alignment of U.S. and Turkish interests elsewhere in the region. This could especially be the case if Turkey-Israel disagreements on Palestinian issues result in future high-profile incidents or if Turkey seeks to actively exclude Israel from regional security arrangements with Egypt or other countries.

In September 2011, diplomatic efforts aimed at getting Israel to apologize to Turkey for the killing of eight Turks and an American of Turkish origin during the May 2010 Gaza flotilla incident reportedly stalled due to Israeli Prime Minister Binyamin Netanyahu's concerns about the potential Israeli public reaction.[40] When the report of the U.N. Secretary-General's panel of inquiry on the incident—also known as the "Palmer Report"[41]—was leaked by the *New York Times* and other outlets, Turkey announced that it was downgrading its diplomatic relations with Israel to the second secretary level—effectively expelling Israel's ambassador to Turkey.[42] It also suspended all Turkey-Israel military agreements. The countries' bilateral free trade agreement remains in effect.

Turkey continues to insist on both an apology and compensation from Israel for families of the Turkish fatalities in return for the possibility of normalization. It also seeks a lifting of the Israeli naval blockade on the Gaza Strip. Erdogan spoke of the possibility of having Turkish naval vessels accompany future aid flotillas to Gaza, but subsequently said that no plans for such voyages were imminent. Erdogan also speculated that international sanctions against Israel could be a source of leverage in solving the Israeli-Palestinian conflict.[43] Though Erdogan supports a negotiated two-state solution to the conflict, he backs Palestinian pursuit of United Nations membership and Fatah-Hamas rapprochement as well.

It is debatable whether an active U.S. brokering role would improve or worsen prospects for Turkey-Israel rapprochement and for future U.S. relations with both countries. In a December 2011 speech, Secretary of Defense Leon Panetta said:

> Like all of you, I've been deeply troubled by the direction of the Turkish-Israeli relationship. Turkey is a key NATO ally and has proven to be a real partner in our effort to support democratic change and stand against authoritarian regimes that use violence against their own people. It is in Israel's interest, Turkey's interest, and U.S. interest, for Israel to reconcile with Turkey. And both Turkey and Israel need to do more to put their relationship back on the right track.[44]

Many analysts have postulated that growing tension between Turkey and Israel could lead to increased congressional opposition to U.S. strategic cooperation with Turkey and perhaps to greater willingness to consider passing a so-called Armenian genocide resolution (see "Possible Armenian Genocide" below).[45] Following the May 2010 flotilla incident, the Senate passed S.Res. 548 by voice vote on June 24, 2010. The resolution condemned the attack by the "extremists aboard the Mavi Marmara," invoked Israel's right to self-defense, and encouraged "the Government of Turkey to recognize the importance of continued strong relations with Israel and the necessity of closely scrutinizing organizations with potential ties to terrorist groups" (a reference to the Turkish Islamist non-governmental organization IHH Humanitarian Relief Foundation, the main organizer of the flotilla).[46] In early 2011, a *New York Times Magazine* article quoted a Turkish diplomat responsible for U.S. relations as saying, "We're getting a lot of flak from the Hill. We used to get hit by the Greek lobby and the Armenian lobby, but we were protected by the Jewish lobby. Now the Jewish lobby is coming after us as well."[47]

Syria[48]

Before civil unrest broke out in Syria in March 2011, Turkey had cultivated close relations with the regime of Syrian President Bashar al Asad by such means as holding joint military exercises, negotiating free trade and no-visa travel agreements, and mediating Syria's indirect talks with Israel in 2008. When unrest began in Syria, Erdogan and other Turkish leaders urged Asad to respond by implementing significant political reforms. Asad's failure to undertake serious reforms and his reliance on violent suppression of demonstrations and targeting of oppositionists led Erdogan to criticize Asad and his tactics with increasing intensity.

Erdogan called on Asad to step down in November 2011, following attacks against Turkish diplomatic installations in Syria by pro-Asad demonstrators and against buses carrying Turkish pilgrims returning from Mecca by regime military forces at a security checkpoint. Foreign Minister Davutoglu subsequently announced multiple military, financial, and diplomatic sanctions against Asad's regime.[49] Turkish leaders reportedly consult frequently on Syria with President Obama and his top national security aides.

Events in Syria have prompted Turkish officials to state that they consider the ongoing unrest a matter of internal Turkish concern, not simply a matter of international affairs. In June 2011, security forces loyal to the Asad regime increasingly targeted alleged outposts of rebel sentiment and activity in northwest Syria near the Turkish border. As a result, over 20,000 refugees fled over the border into temporary camps maintained by Turkey.

Over half of these returned to Syria, but additional refugee flows in late 2011 and early 2012 have brought the current number to approximately 9,200.[50] Turkey also now serves as a base for exiled leaders in both the Syrian National Council (SNC) and the Free Syrian Army (FSA). The SNC aims to offer a clear political alternative to Asad for the international community, while the FSA is comprised of defectors from Syria's security forces who may be seeking to lead an armed insurrection against the Asad regime. Turkish officials maintain that they do not support violent means of opposition.

Turkey's increasing embrace of the Syrian opposition while Asad remains in power entails risks for Turkey. It also could further antagonize Iran—with possible implications for regional developments in Iraq, Lebanon, and elsewhere. Some reports state that Turkish officials might consider using military means to establish and maintain a buffer zone in northern Syria under an international mandate supported by the Arab League and United Nations Security Council.

A buffer zone—similar to the one Turkey established in northern Iraq during the 1991 Gulf War— could provide a place of refuge for endangered Syrian citizens without involving Turkish territory. However, it also could be a staging area for defectors and oppositionists—possibly with future Turkish and other external assistance—to mount an armed campaign against the Asad regime, similar to the role eastern Libya played for the NATO-backed opposition forces that toppled the Qadhafi regime in 2011. When asked at a December 14, 2011, hearing of the House Foreign Affairs Subcommittee on the Middle East and South Asia to describe Turkey's support for the Syrian opposition, Frederic Hof, Special Coordinator for Regional Affairs at the State Department, said:

> Turkey has provided shelter to the Free Syrian Army. What the Turks tell us, and we have no reason to disbelieve them, is that they are not arming these folks and sending them across into Syria. That is—that is their position. We have no reason to disbelieve it.
>
> I am sure that—that Turkey is examining many, many, many different options and contingencies right now, based on a variety of scenarios that—that could come up. I am not aware of any near-term plans, you know, to establish safe zones or whatever on Syrian territory.

Some analysts have expressed concern that the AKP government's potential influence with the SNC and FSA could exacerbate sectarian animus between Syria's majority Sunnis and ruling minority Alawites.

They also worry it could skew the relative influence of various groups within the Syrian opposition in favor of the Muslim Brotherhood and to the detriment of Syrian Kurds. Reports indicate that Asad might possibly be seeking to placate Syrian Kurds' opposition to his regime while simultaneously encouraging PKK terrorist activity in Turkey by granting Kurds greater autonomy in Syria's northeast.[51]

Iran and NATO Missile Defense

In September 2011, Turkey agreed to host a U.S. forward-deployed early warning radar at the Kurecik base near the eastern Turkish city of Malatya as part of a NATO-approved missile defense system that most analysts believe is intended to counter potential ballistic missile threats to Europe from Iran.[52] A senior U.S. Administration official called this agreement "probably the biggest strategic decision between the United States and Turkey in the past 15 or 20 years."[53] Some Iranian officials, after initially expressing displeasure with Turkey's decision, have stated that Iran would target the radar in Turkey in the event of a U.S. or Israeli airstrike on Iran. CNN reported in January 2012 that a Turkish foreign ministry official announced that the radar has been activated.[54]

The decision to host the missile defense radar was made within the context of a region with shifting dynamics. Differing Iranian and Turkish interests in the region have led to increased competition for influence over developments in Iraq and Syria, and for the admiration of Arab populations on issues such as championing the Palestinian cause. Turkey's renewed closeness with the United States has further fueled Turkey-Iran tensions at a time when the Obama Administration is continuing its efforts to isolate Iran because of its nuclear program and its support for various actors seen as destabilizing forces in the region.

Yet, Turkish officials continue to stress the importance of good relations with Iran and meet regularly with Iranian counterparts, in the interests of maintaining stability and trade, and also to keep open the possibility of mediating the international impasse on Iran's nuclear program. Following some reports that Iran might be assisting the PKK, Iran and Turkey publicly committed in October 2011 to cooperating against the PKK and the Iranian Kurdish separatist organization Party of Free Life of Kurdistan (PJAK) that also maintains safe havens in northern Iraq. Turkey has stated that it will comply with the U.N. sanctions against Iran that it voted against in 2010 (as opposed to U.S. and EU sanctions, which are not binding on it). Turkish officials still plan to boost trade with Iran from approximately $15 billion to $30 billion a year by 2015. Iran accounts for at least 30% of Turkey's oil imports. To safeguard its energy trade with Iran, reports indicate that Turkey, along with other countries such as Japan and South Korea, may be seeking an exemption from the Obama Administration from U.S. sanctions enacted at the end of 2011 under the 2012 National Defense Authorization Act (P.L. 112-81).[55] These sanctions, which target financial institutions that deal with Iran's central bank and are seen as aimed at Iran's oil export business, might otherwise apply to oil import transactions involving the major Turkish refinery Tupras and Turkish public lenders.[56]

Iraq and the PKK

Turkey cooperated with the United States in the 1991 Gulf War and following the U.S.-led 2003 Iraq invasion, but the Turkish parliamentary decision in 2003 not to allow U.S. forces to use its territory to open a northern front significantly affected U.S.-Turkey relations. The decision showed the United States that in its strategic relationship with Turkey, it could no longer rely solely on past legacies of cooperation and its close ties with the Turkish military.[57] Starting in late 2007, U.S. willingness to provide greater counterterrorism support to Turkey in its struggle against the PKK helped move U.S.-Turkey priorities in Iraq toward greater alignment.

For Turkey, strong governance and stability in Iraq is important particularly due to Turkish interests in denying the PKK use of Iraqi territory for its safe havens; discouraging the cross-border spread of Kurdish separatist sentiment; countering Iranian influence; and accessing Iraq's potentially lucrative export markets and ample energy resources (which could eventually lessen Turkey's dependence on Iranian and Russian energy imports). U.S. officials have repeatedly expressed appreciation for Turkey's constructive role in post-conflict Iraq, with which it has growing trade and where it has improved relations with the Kurdish Regional Government. Turkey's role in Iraq is likely to become more significant in light of the U.S. military mission's transition in Iraq to a civilian security assistance mission at the end of 2011.

Clashes between Turkish forces and the PKK intensified following Turkish national elections in June 2011. The PKK's renewed resort to violence might be motivated by a number of factors, including the example of insurgencies in Arab countries throughout the region, a desire to take advantage of the fluidity of the regional turmoil, and a hope to gain greater support for Kurdish rights in the domestic political and constitutional debate among Turkish lawmakers and citizens. The PKK and individuals and groups believed to be affiliated with it have carried out multiple attacks on both military and civilian targets. As a result, Turkey has increased air and artillery attacks on PKK safe havens in Iraq, aided by intelligence-sharing from the United States, and has reportedly involved ground forces across the border as well. Given its military drawdown from Iraq, the United States is now reportedly basing the unarmed Predator drone aircraft that it uses to gather intelligence on the PKK at Turkey's Incirlik air base.[58] Other reports indicate that Prime Minister Erdogan has reiterated Turkey's desire to purchase drones (including some with armed capability) from the United States for its own use. Such purchases would likely require congressional notification (see "Arms Sales and Military/Security Assistance" below).[59]

Table 3. PKK Designations by U.S. Government

Designation	Year
Foreign Terrorist Organization	1997
Specially Designated Global Terrorist	2001
Significant Foreign Narcotics Trafficker	2008

Cyprus and the Eastern Mediterranean[60]

Since Cyprus became independent of the United Kingdom in 1960, Turkey has viewed itself and has acted as the protector of the island's ethnic Turkish minority out of concerns over its treatment by the ethnic Greek majority.[61] Responding to Greek and Cypriot political developments that raised concerns about a possible Greek annexation of Cyprus, Turkey's military intervened in 1974[62] and established control over the northern third of the island, prompting an almost total ethnic and de facto political division along geographical lines. That division persists today and is the subject of continuing international efforts aimed at reunification.[63] The ethnic Greek-ruled Republic of Cyprus is internationally recognized as having jurisdiction over the entire island, while the de facto Turkish Republic of Northern Cyprus in the northern third has only Turkish recognition.

The Republic of Cyprus's accession to the EU in 2004, and Turkey's refusal to normalize political and commercial relations with it is seen as a major obstacle to Turkey's EU membership aspirations. It also hinders effective EU-NATO defense cooperation. EU accession also may have reduced incentives for Cyprus's Greek population to make concessions toward a reunification deal. The Greek Cypriots rejected by referendum a United Nations plan (called the Annan plan after then Secretary-General Kofi Annan) in 2004 that the Turkish Cypriot population accepted. Turkey and Turkish Cypriot leaders claim that the Turkish Cypriot regime's lack of international recognition unfairly denies its people basic economic and political rights, particularly through barriers to trade with and travel to countries other than Turkey.

Turkey has assertively opposed efforts by the Republic of Cyprus and other Eastern Mediterranean countries—most notably Israel—to agree upon a division of offshore energy drilling rights before Cyprus's political future is resolved. In response to drilling initiated in September 2011 by the Republic of Cyprus in the Aphrodite gas field off Cyprus's southern coast, Turkey sent its own seismic research ships with a naval escort to waters off the Cypriot shore in agreement with the Turkish Cypriot regime.[64] Turkey and the Turkish Cypriots oppose Greek Cypriot drilling without a solution to the larger question of the island's unification. Turkish Energy Minister Taner Yildiz announced plans in November 2011 for the state-run Turkish Petroleum Corporation (TPAO) to begin land drilling for oil and natural gas in northern Cyprus.

Turkey and the Turkish Cypriot regime have indicated that their openness to continued unification talks will end in July 2012 if the Republic of Cyprus assumes the rotating EU presidency as it is currently slated to do. The United States has voiced concern about tensions in the Eastern Mediterranean, particularly because the Greek Cypriot drilling is being conducted by Texas company Noble Energy. According to one source, Prime Minister Erdogan told President Obama in September 2011 that Turkish ships would not interfere with Greek Cypriot drilling.[65]

Armenia[66]

In late 2009, Turkey and Armenia, aided by Swiss mediation, agreed to joint protocols that would have normalized relations and opened borders between the two countries. They also would have called for a dialogue and impartial examination of the historical record with respect to "existing problems," widely believed to refer to the issue of World War I-era deaths of hundreds of thousands of Armenians through the actions of Ottoman Empire authorities. Turkish leaders were unwilling to push for parliamentary ratification of the protocols, however, due to Azerbaijani objections to Turkey-Armenia normalization prior to desired progress on the issue of Nagorno-Karabakh.[67] Azerbaijan influences Turkish policy on this issue because of its close cultural and economic ties with Turkey, particularly as Azerbaijan is a key energy supplier. Another possible cause for Turkish reluctance was a 2010 Armenian constitutional court ruling that indicated inflexibility on the genocide issue. Subsequently, Turkey and Armenia have made little or no progress toward ratifying the protocols or otherwise normalizing their relations, though the protocols remain under consideration in Turkey's parliament.[68] In December 2011, Turkish media reported that Foreign Minister Davutoglu had consulted with Swiss officials to determine prospects for reviving talks aimed at normalization in the event of Armenia-Azerbaijan progress on Nagorno-Karabakh.[69] The tenor of relations between Turkey and Armenia could be an important factor in a potential congressional debate over a future genocide resolution.

Afghanistan

Turkey has twice commanded the International Security Assistance Force (ISAF) in Afghanistan and has had troops participating in ISAF since shortly after its inception in December 2001. Turkey's approximately 2,000 troops concentrate on training Afghan military and security forces and providing security in Kabul, where Turkey commands ISAF's Regional Command-Capital, as well as in Wardak (just west of Kabul) and Jawzjan (in northern Afghanistan) provinces.[70] In addition, some Afghan police are trained in Turkey.

As with several other NATO and non-NATO contributors to ISAF, Turkey's troops are not involved in combat. Turkey's history of good relations with both Afghanistan and Pakistan and its status as the Muslim-majority country with the greatest level of involvement in ISAF are thought by some analysts to help legitimize ISAF's presence. These relations could become more important to preparing Afghanistan for stable, self-sufficient rule, with the United States and other ISAF countries scheduled to wind down their military presence in Afghanistan in future years.

Regional Energy Issues

Turkey as a Transit Corridor and Potential Source[71]

Turkey's role as a regional energy transport corridor is growing, particularly with respect to natural gas. With supply sources that include Russia, Iran, other littoral Caspian Sea states, and— potentially—Iraq, the importance of Turkey's security for world energy markets has increased.

Turkey's location has made it a key country in the U.S. and European effort to establish a southern corridor for natural gas transit from diverse sources.[72]

In October 2011, Azerbaijan and Turkey reached final terms for the transit of Azerbaijan's Shah Deniz Phase 2 natural gas through the southern corridor. The terms specified that 565 billion-700 billion cubic feet (bcf) of natural gas would transit Turkey, of which 210 bcf would be available for Turkey's domestic use.

Recent announcements of significant natural gas resources in the Eastern Mediterranean have prompted Turkey to get involved. State-run TPAO has agreed to assist the de facto Turkish Cypriot regime with oil and gas exploration in northern Cyprus, and is pursuing deals with international companies for exploration in and off the coast of Turkey. It is unclear whether these efforts will produce substantial energy finds. It is also unclear whether they will lead to greater political conflict with other countries newly active in Eastern Mediterranean energy exploration—particularly Israel and the Republic of Cyprus, both of which have already made sizeable natural gas discoveries.

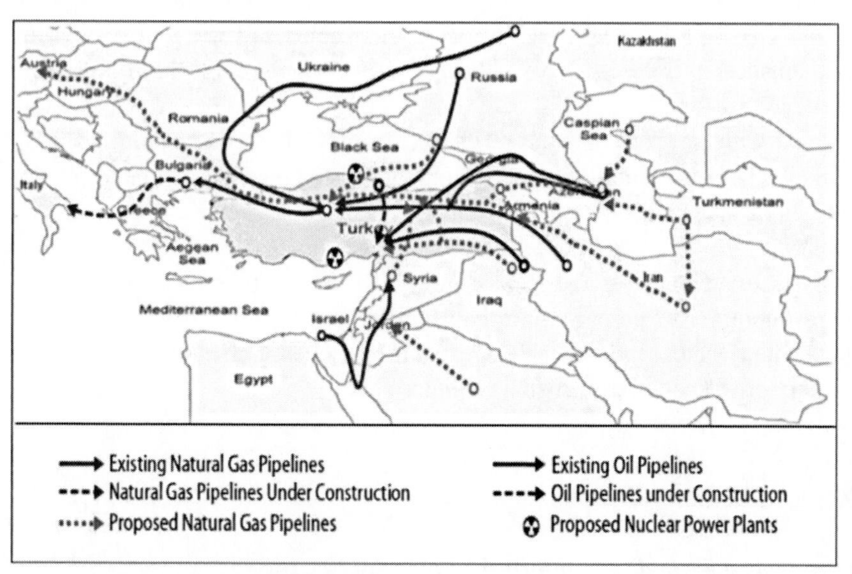

Source: Turkish Economic Ministry, adapted by CRS.
Notes: All locations are approximate.

Figure 2. Major Pipelines Traversing Turkey and Possible Nuclear Power Plants, (as of September 2011).

Nuclear Energy

Turkey has had plans for establishing nuclear power generation since 1970 but still does not have any active plants. After carrying out feasibility studies for potential sites, initial efforts to attract tenders from international companies foundered in the 1980s and 1990s due to multiple factors. These included a lack of adequate financing and environmental concerns exacerbated by the 1986 Chernobyl disaster.

Given rapidly increasing rates of consumption amid robust Turkish economic growth, environmental and other political objections to nuclear power may no longer outweigh its appeal as a potentially plentiful, locally produced energy source. In addition, the fractious Turkish ruling coalitions of earlier decades have given way to AKP government leaders seemingly confident in their electoral mandate. They portray Turkey's pursuit of nuclear energy as a matter of national self-reliance and prestige.[73]

In June 2008, the United States and Turkey signed a 15-year "123 Agreement" for peaceful nuclear cooperation in line with international nuclear non-proliferation norms.[74] The nature of future U.S.-Turkey cooperation under this agreement is likely to depend in part on whether, when, and how Turkey constructs and operates nuclear power plants in partnership with international companies. In May 2010, Turkey signed an agreement with Rosatom—Russia's state-run nuclear company—to have it form a subsidiary to build, own, and operate Turkey's first nuclear power plant for an estimated $20 billion, to be located in Akkuyu near the Mediterranean port of Mersin. Despite the proposed plant's location near an earthquake fault line, Turkey and Rosatom reportedly plan to stay with a timetable that has construction beginning in 2012-2013 and operations beginning in 2019, even after the global concerns raised by the Fukushima Daiichi meltdown following the March 2011 earthquake/tsunami in Japan. Given that construction at Akkuyu has been postponed multiple times since the location was approved by Turkey in 1976, skepticism over the viability of the proposed plant might persist up to and even after operations begin. In addition to financial or technical obstacles, political controversy could revive over geological or environmental concerns, and proponents of diversification could increasingly oppose construction of a plant that might further Turkey's energy dependence on Russia. Turkey is reportedly considering a contract with a Japanese company to build a second nuclear power plant in the northern town of Sinop on the Black Sea coast.[75]

The full range of motivations underlying Turkey's potential use of nuclear energy is unclear, though many analysts express confidence that Turkish decision-making on the issue is significantly influenced by regional security considerations. One has written:

> At this point, little evidence exists to suggest that Turkey's nuclear energy goals are tied to future plans for weaponization. Nevertheless, it is clear that Turkey's nuclear program, no matter how explicitly "peaceful," is ultimately strategic in nature. Either by relieving Ankara of its dependence on foreign energy supplies or providing a hedge against potential longterm security threats, Turkey's nuclear program has been designed with its neighbors clearly in mind.[76]

Turkey and the European Union[77]

The Turkish government uses its demographic profile to support a bid for EU membership, arguing that it would bring a young, dynamic population to the aging ranks of Europe and boost EU influence in the Muslim world. Turkey first sought to associate itself with the then European Economic Community (EEC) in 1959, and Turkey and the EEC entered into an agreement of association in 1963. EU accession talks, which began in 2005, have been stalled owing to the opposition of key EU states—most notably France and Germany—to Turkey's full membership.

Opponents generally articulate empirical rationales for their positions, but many analysts believe that resistance to Turkish EU accession is rooted in fear that Turkey's large Muslim population would fundamentally change the cultural character of the EU and dilute the power of the EU's founding Western European states to drive the policy agenda.

Since 1995, Turkey has had a full customs union with the EU. It also is a member of the Council of Europe, along with several other non-EU states (including Russia), and is subject to the jurisdiction of the Council's European Court of Human Rights. Waning domestic expectations of and support for full accession to the EU, along with fundamental concerns over the economic and political soundness of the EU given the ongoing eurozone crisis, have contributed to an environment in which Turkish leaders, including Prime Minister Erdogan, now proclaim that the EU may need Turkey more than Turkey needs the EU.[78] As mentioned above, Turkey's unwillingness to normalize diplomatic and trade relations with EU member Cyprus presents a major obstacle to its accession prospects.[79] Other EU concerns over Turkey's qualifications for membership center on the treatment of Kurds and religious minorities, media freedoms, women's rights, and the proper and transparent functioning of Turkey's democratic and legal systems.[80] Nevertheless, the EU provides over $1 billion in annual pre-accession financial and technical assistance to Turkey aimed at harmonizing its economy, society, bureaucracy, and political system with those of EU members.[81]

Other International Relationships

As Turkey continues to exercise increased political and economic influence, it seeks to establish and strengthen relationships with non-Western global powers. It is expanding trade and defense industrial ties with China, Russia, and other countries in Asia and Africa. Turkey also has held joint military exercises with China on Turkish soil.

Turkey additionally seeks to expand the scope of its regional influence, with its officials sometimes comparing its historical links and influence with certain countries—especially former territories of the Ottoman Empire—to the relationship of Britain with its commonwealth. Through hands-on political involvement, as well as increased private trade and investment and public humanitarian and development projects, Turkey has enhanced its influence and image as a leading Muslim-majority democracy with Muslim-populated countries not only in the Middle East, but also in the Balkans, the Caucasus and Central Asia, and sub-Saharan Africa.[82]

U.S.-TURKEY RELATIONS

Overview

The United States and Turkey have enjoyed a decades-long alliance dating from the onset of the Cold War. At the outset of the Obama Administration, U.S. officials made clear their intent to emphasize the importance of a multifaceted strategic relationship with Turkey. Subsequent bilateral and NATO-related developments during the Obama Administration have led to questions about the extent to which U.S. and Turkish strategic priorities and values converge on both a short- and long-term basis.

In April 2009, President Obama, speaking of a "model partnership," visited Turkey during his first presidential trip abroad and addressed the Parliament in Ankara, saying that "Turkey is a critical ally.... And Turkey and the United States must stand together—and work together—to overcome the challenges of our time." One month later, Ahmet Davutoglu, a foreign policy academic-turned-advisor to Prime Minister Erdogan, became Turkey's foreign minister, giving Davutoglu greater visibility with regard to the more independent and assertive Turkish foreign policy course he had helped to establish when the AKP came to power in 2002. His course envisions Turkey being "in the centre of its own sphere of influence" through "strategic depth" based largely on regional soft power through geopolitical, cultural, historical, and economic influence, and having "zero problems" with the countries in its vicinity.[83]

Subsequent Turkish and U.S. actions and statements on Armenia, Iran, and Israeli-Palestinian issues revealed tensions between the Obama Administration and AKP government visions for overcoming regional challenges. A vote in March 2010 by the House Committee on Foreign Affairs to report H.Res. 252 on the question of a possible Armenian genocide for consideration by the full House led Turkey to temporarily recall its ambassador.

Then, in May and June 2010, two developments raised significant concerns regarding U.S.- Turkey relations:

1) Turkey's Iranian nuclear diplomacy with Brazil—the Tehran Declaration on possible nuclear fuel swaps, followed by the Turkey-Brazil "no" vote on U.N. Security Council enhanced sanctions on Iran in Resolution 1929.
2) The *Mavi Marmara* Gaza flotilla incident and its aftermath

Some Members of Congress and Administration officials, viewing Turkey's rhetoric and actions as (1) undermining a top U.S. priority in the Iranian nuclear issue and (2) being at odds with the U.S. characterization of Israel as an ally and Iran as a threat, openly questioned Turkey's orientation on global security issues. Philip Gordon, U.S. Assistant Secretary of State for European and Eurasian Affairs, said in June 2010,

> We think Turkey remains committed to NATO, Europe and the United States, but that needs to be demonstrated. There are people asking questions about it in a way that is new, and that in itself is a bad thing that makes it harder for the United States to support some of the things that Turkey would like to see us support.[84]

Officials' and analysts' questions about Turkey's foreign policy direction intensified following reports that the 2010 version of the Turkish National Security Policy Document (also known as the "Red Book") downgraded or did not explicitly list possible threats from Iran, Syria, Greece, and Armenia that were listed in previous versions. At the same time, the Red Book reportedly defined Israel's actions in the region as a threat—claiming that they induce conditions of instability.[85]

As discussed above, however, in 2011 concerns about the compatibility of U.S. and Turkish strategic priorities and values were partly allayed by shared U.S.-Turkey interests in promoting democratic transition in the Middle East and in preventing actors such as Iran from exacerbating regional sectarian tensions and security dilemmas.

Many U.S. observers have criticized Erdogan and Davutoglu for perceived double standards and selective implementation of Turkey's stated zero-problem foreign policy. Erdogan has adamantly denounced Israel's treatment of Palestinians, especially in the Gaza Strip, and has suggested that international sanctions against Israel could help end the stalemate in the Arab-Israeli peace process.

Yet, he has met with Hamas leaders in Turkey and has dubbed its members "resistance fighters" instead of terrorists; he was one of the first world leaders to congratulate Iranian President Mahmoud Ahmadinejad on his disputed reelection in June 2009; and he has said in defending Sudanese President Omar al Bashir regarding allegations from Darfur and elsewhere that it is "not possible for those who belong to the Muslim faith to carry out genocide."

Even as events in 2011 have led Turkey to coordinate more closely with its U.S. and other NATO allies, Erdogan has questioned their positions and/or motivations.[86] Though Erdogan supports a two-state solution to the Israeli-Palestinian conflict, he routinely criticizes the U.S.-led approach to the peace process in the international media.

One U.S. analyst has asserted that Erdogan's rhetoric and actions are largely calculated to appeal to and influence Turkish domestic public opinion.[87]

A late 2010 poll indicated that despite the longtime U.S.-Turkey alliance, and despite several potential threats along Turkey's borders, a plurality of Turks see the United States as Turkey's biggest external threat.[88] This sentiment exists within a context of Turks' generally low favorability ratings for foreign countries, partly based on historical concerns about encirclement by outside powers—particularly the West and Russia.

However, an early 2011 poll indicated improvements in Turkish perceptions of U.S. influence in the world.[89]

Bilateral and NATO Defense Cooperation[90]

The U.S.-Turkey alliance has long centered on the countries' defense relationship, both bilaterally and within NATO. With several challenges to U.S. national security emanating from the greater Middle East, Turkey is arguably a more significant ally for the United States at present than during the Cold War. Turkey's location near several global hotspots makes the continuing availability of its territory for the stationing and transport of arms, cargo, and personnel valuable for the United States and NATO. Announcements during 2011 that Turkey would host the early warning missile defense radar and that NATO would transform its air command center in Izmir into a ground forces command center while closing land bases in Germany and Spain have reinforced Turkey's strategic importance for the alliance.

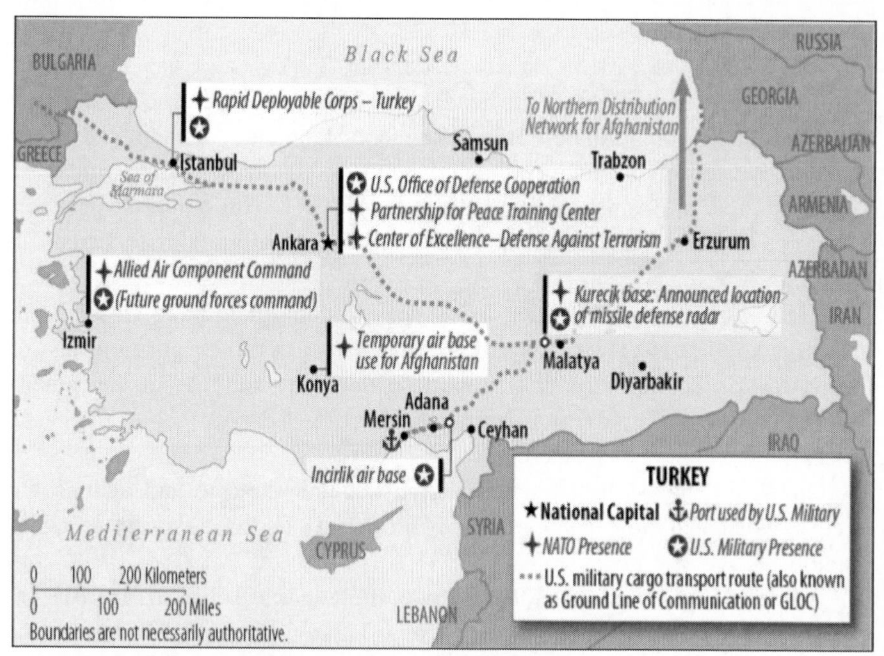

Source: Department of Defense, NATO; adapted by CRS

Notes: All locations are approximate. Incirlik air base is a Turkish base, part of which is used for limited purposes by the U.S. military. Additional information on the U.S./NATO military presence in Turkey is available in CRS Report R41761, *Turkey-U.S. Defense Cooperation: Prospects and Challenges*, by Jim Zanotti.

Figure 3. Map of U.S. and NATO Military Presence and Transport Routes in Turkey.

Although the Turkish military remains the most trusted institution in the country and retains greater power in the political process than most (if not all) of its NATO counterparts, its decline in influence in the last decade has led many observers to conclude that the military's traditional role as the primary interlocutor for the United States and other NATO allies is in jeopardy, if not already obsolete. Adjusting to changes in the Turkish civil-military power structure presents a challenge for U.S. officials in adjusting future modes of bilateral interaction. It might lead to an approach that is more multi-dimensional than the well-established pattern some observers see in which the State Department and other U.S. officials rely on the "Pentagon to wield its influence."[91]

Since 1948, the United States has provided Turkey with approximately $13.8 billion in overall military assistance. Current annual military and security assistance, however, is limited to approximately $6 million annually in International Military Education and Training (IMET); International Narcotics Control and Law Enforcement (INCLE); and Nonproliferation, Antiterrorism, Demining and Related Programs (NADR) funds. This assistance facilitates U.S.- Turkey counterterrorism cooperation against Al Qaeda and other worldwide terrorist networks.

Table 4. U.S. Foreign Assistance to Turkey ($ in millions)

Account	FY2010	FY2011	FY2012
International Military Education and Training (IMET)	5.0	4.0	4.0
International Narcotics Control and Law Enforcement (INCLE)	--	0.5	0.5
Nonproliferation, Antiterrorism, Demining, and Related Programs (NADR)	3.0	1.4	1.1
Total	8.0	5.9	5.6

Source: U.S. Department of State.

Note: All amounts are approximate.

POSSIBLE U.S. POLICY OPTIONS

Although U.S. and Turkish interests and policies intersect in many respects, Turkey's growing regional influence and military, economic, and political self-reliance have decreased its dependence on the United States. The appeal of U.S. and Western power, prestige, values, and military technology might currently outstrip that of potential competitors, but Turkish actions might be affected by possible perceptions of decreasing U.S. global and regional preeminence. Given the impact Turkey has and potentially could have on a number of major U.S. priorities, a prescriptive approach that defines the U.S. relationship with Turkey in terms of one or two specific issues may have negative repercussions for cooperation on matters of significant U.S. interest.

Members of Congress might consider maintaining or initiating active congressional inquiry into and coordinating with Obama Administration positions on Turkey. U.S. policymakers might consider cultivating other NATO and Middle Eastern allies whose cooperation will increase the attractiveness for Turkey of cooperation with the United States. One U.S. analyst wrote in December 2011:

> Despite record levels of communication and travel between top leaders in Ankara and Washington, the societal and institutional connections are still in need of revitalization and strengthening.... [C]oordination and policy on Turkey continues to affect vital interests throughout Washington, which ideally must go beyond the administration to the Hill and society at large even if there is short-term turbulence.[92]

Although short-term prospects may not be favorable for Turkish accession to the European Union, U.S. support for eventual Turkish EU membership, supplemented by U.S. consultations with Turkey and EU actors on the use of pre-accession aid and other means of increasing TurkeyEU harmonization, could help further anchor Turkey's domestic and foreign policies within the West. However, if U.S. policymakers believe that an open-ended EU accession process in the face of current obstacles to Turkish membership is counterproductive, they might discuss alternative or parallel courses of action in hopes of maximizing the benefits of the U.S.-Turkey alliance on the issues discussed below.

Influencing Regional Change and Promoting Stability

Turkey is likely to play a key role in affecting the outcomes of ongoing political change and unrest in the broader Middle East, including Iraq and Afghanistan as both countries transition from U.S.-led military occupation to greater self-rule. In partnering with Turkey to influence regional change and promote stability, the following options are available for Members of Congress and Obama Administration officials to adopt or continue:

- Determine whether and how to discourage further deterioration in Turkey's relations with Israel. For example, should the United States mediate Turkey-Israel security understandings and encourage either a discreet or a more public Turkey-Israel rapprochement? Policymakers could condition various modes of U.S. cooperation with Turkey on its relations with Israel, but this could lead Turkey to decrease its overall cooperation with the United States and increasingly look to other countries to address its demands.
- Determine the proper nature and extent of bilateral and NATO military and intelligence cooperation, including joint use of Turkish bases and territory, as well as information sharing to assist in countering the PKK and in facilitating interdiction of illegal arms shipments from other countries or non-state actors.
- Determine whether and how to encourage Turkish political and financial support for individuals and groups opposing autocratic regimes, and whether and how such backing should be linked to support for democratically accountable and economically viable transitions in countries experiencing unrest or leadership changes.
- Determine whether and how to coordinate with Turkey to impose and enforce unilateral, multilateral, or international sanctions (diplomatic, military, and/or economic) that have the potential to effectively weaken or change the behavior of regimes or other actors violating human rights or otherwise contravening international laws and norms. Examples include the Asad regime in Syria for violently suppressing popular protest and the Iranian regime for its nuclear program and support of regional terrorist groups.
- Determine whether and how to support Turkish efforts to coordinate regional security with other local actors, especially other U.S. allies.

Action on any of these options will take place in a complex regional and strategic environment whose trajectory has probably become more unpredictable in the past year, perhaps increasing the difficulty of calculating risks and determining probable outcomes.

Arms Sales and Military/Security Assistance

Turkey continues to seek advanced U.S. military equipment (i.e., fighter aircraft, drone aircraft, helicopters, and missile defense systems), and its defense industry participates in joint ventures with the United States (e.g., on the F-35 Joint Strike Fighter). However, Turkey's growing defense industry and its increased willingness to engage in arms import-export transactions or joint military exercises with non-NATO countries, such as China, Russia, Pakistan, and South Korea, indicate Turkey's interest in diversifying its defense relationships and decreasing its dependence on the United States. U.S. military and security assistance programs for Turkey are designed to cultivate closeness in relationships and practices between Turkish military officers and security officials and their U.S. counterparts.

Turkey is particularly interested in acquiring armed drones from the United States to use against the PKK. It has reportedly sought to purchase four MQ-1 Predator drones and six MQ-9 Reaper drones (more advanced versions of the Predator) since 2008.[93] In September 2011, according to Turkish media outlet *Today's Zaman*, Prime Minister Erdogan claimed that Turkey had reached agreement in principle with the Obama Administration to either lease or purchase U.S. drones, and Turkish Defense Minister Ismet Yilmaz subsequently announced that delivery was expected in June 2012,[94] though this has not been publicly confirmed or denied by U.S. officials. In October 2011, the Administration notified Congress of a possible $111 million Foreign Military Sale to Turkey of three AH-1W SuperCobra attack helicopters from the U.S. Marine Corps inventory. Though Representative Shelley Berkley introduced a joint resolution on November 3, 2011 (H.J.Res. 83)—co-sponsored by 12 Members—proposing disapproval of the sale, the 15- day notification period elapsed without congressional action to delay or block the potential sale, allowing it to go forward.

Lack of effective opposition from Congress on the helicopter sale could signal a general willingness to support Turkish priorities in countering terrorism and stabilizing Iraq given the U.S. military drawdown and in light of Turkey's seeming willingness to oppose Iran on issues such as the NATO missile defense radar and the future of Syria. Nevertheless, reports have indicated that some Members of Congress have balked at the drone sale.[95] In October 2011, Assistant Secretary of Defense for International Security Affairs Alexander Vershbow reportedly said in a speech to the American-Turkish Council, "This topic is influenced by the problems in Turkish-Israeli relations. This is not a secret. But just to repeat it, we do support the sale."[96] Concerns about sensitive technology transfer might also exist that are less applicable to the helicopter sale, partly because Turkey already possesses some SuperCobras. With the region's stability in question, one could additionally question whether drones initially intended to fight the PKK in Turkey and possibly Iraq could be used in the future for other purposes. By redeploying the four U.S. Predator drones from Iraq to Turkey in late 2011,[97] the Obama Administration might have bought time for further consultations with Congress on a potential drone sale.

Possible Armenian Genocide

Congress's involvement on Turkey-Armenia issues has the potential to strongly influence U.S.- Turkey relations. In March 2010 during the 111th Congress, the House Committee on Foreign Affairs voted to report H.Res. 252 for consideration by the full House (by a vote of 23-22). H.Res. 252 characterized actions of the Ottoman Empire against Armenians from 1915 to 1917 as genocide. Similar resolutions had been reported multiple times by congressional committees since 1984 (see Appendix C for a full list), and President Ronald Reagan referred to a "genocide of the Armenians" during a Holocaust Remembrance Day speech in 1981.

H.Res. 252 did not pass, but in response to the March 2010 committee action, Turkey recalled its ambassador from the United States for one month, and at least one prominent AKP lawmaker reportedly warned that "the relationship would be downgraded on every level" in the event of House passage of the resolution. This warning was commonly interpreted as including a threat to curtail at least partially or temporarily U.S. access to Turkish bases and territory for transporting non-lethal cargo to missions in Iraq and Afghanistan.[98] Representative Robert Dold introduced H.Res. 304—virtually identical to H.Res. 252—in June 2011 during the 112th Congress. The proposed resolution has garnered over 85 co-sponsors and has been referred to the House Committee on Foreign Affairs.

At least 20 countries other than Armenia have recognized the Ottoman-era deaths as genocide in some way, including 11 of the 27 EU member states.[99] France is one of these countries, and in January 2012, the French Senate passed legislation that, if signed by President Nicolas Sarkozy, would criminalize denial of an Armenian genocide. Following passage of the legislation in the parliament's lower house in December 2011, Prime Minister Erdogan recalled Turkey's ambassador from France and halted all Turkey-France diplomatic consultations and military dealings. In the immediate aftermath of the Senate vote, Turkish leaders have promised "permanent sanctions" against France, which also may increase tensions related to Turkey's EU accession process.[100]

Bilateral Trade Promotion

Although successive U.S. Administrations have cited the importance of increased trade with Turkey, and the Obama Administration has reemphasized this in articulating its vision for a multifaceted bilateral strategic relationship with Turkey, it is unclear how effective government efforts to promote U.S.-Turkey trade can be. A Department of Commerce official told CRS that total U.S.-Turkey trade volume is growing (estimating $20 billion for 2011, an approximate 45% increase from 2010), and said that Turkish exports to the United States are growing faster than exports to the rest of the world.[101] As mentioned above, the United States is Turkey's fourth-largest trading partner, and according to the Department of Commerce, Turkey ranks 26th among countries to which the United States exports merchandise and 47th among countries from which it imports goods.

Table 5. U.S. Merchandise Trade with Turkey ($ in Millions)

	2007	2008	2009	2010
Exports	6,500	9,960	7,090	10,550
Imports	4,600	4,640	3,660	4,200
Total Volume	11,100	14,600	10,750	14,750

Source: U.S. Department of Commerce, Foreign Trade Division, U.S. Bureau of Census.

Both U.S. and Turkish officials repeatedly state their desire to enhance bilateral trade and investment ties. The two countries signed a Trade and Investment Framework Agreement in 1999. Annual meetings for the U.S.-Turkey Framework for Strategic Economic and Commercial Cooperation began in 2010 at the cabinet ministerial level. The goal of the Framework is to intensify bilateral economic relations in a wide range of areas. One current project is the Near-Zero Zone, a public-private partnership initiative which seeks to incentivize U.S. investment in efforts to increase the capacity and efficiency of Turkish energy companies located in Izmir. The U.S. government has designated Turkey as a priority market and the interagency Trade Policy Coordination Commission has developed an Export Enhancement Strategy for Turkey.[102] Additionally, in the 112th Congress, H.R. 2362 (the Indian Tribal Trade and Investment Demonstration Project Act of 2011) was ordered to be reported by the House Natural Resources Committee in November 2011. If enacted, this bill would ease the process by which Turkish companies could do business on American Indian reservations.

U.S. and Turkish advocates for expanded bilateral, non-defense trade seek greater private sector contacts and information campaigns facilitated by government officials—including Members of Congress—through business delegations and contact groups in fields such as energy, property development, high tech engineering and construction, medical supplies, systems management, and marketing.[103] Turkish officials have occasionally proposed a U.S.-Turkey preferential trade agreement[104] or U.S. legislation establishing quailfied industrial zones (QIZs) in Turkey without success. Some policymakers and observers claim that even if past economic conditions may have limited U.S. trade with Turkey, recent growth in Turkish consumer demand, quality of products and services, and global competitiveness and brand recognition have increased Turkey's value as an import source, target market, and place of investment for U.S. companies.[105] The Turkish Ministry of Economy has identified six U.S. states as the focus of its efforts to increase bilateral trade: California, Texas, New York, Florida, Illinois, and Georgia.[106]

CONCLUSION

Turkey's importance to the United States appears to be growing both because of its increasing economic and political influence and because the United States is relying increasingly on Turkey to support U.S. interests in the Middle East as Washington seeks a more economical military and aid strategy. The feasibility of U.S. reliance on Turkey is likely to be tested in relation to developments in Syria, Iraq, and Iran, where U.S.-Turkey interests appear to be more aligned than they were a year ago. Closeness between U.S. and Turkish interests remains subject to fluctuation as events develop, particularly with regard to Turkey's troubled relations with Israel and concerns over strategic preeminence and energy exploration in the Eastern Mediterranean. Congressional action on the possible sale of drone aircraft to Turkey to counter the PKK or on a potential Armenian genocide resolution could significantly affect U.S.-Turkey relations, particularly if Members of Congress link their stances on these issues to the state of Turkey-Israel relations.

The positions Members of Congress take on specific issues concerning Turkey—including defense cooperation, trade promotion, and Turkish domestic developments—also will indicate U.S. priorities at a critical time for global and regional stability and for the Turkish republic's political and constitutional evolution. This could influence Turkish leaders' future foreign policy rhetoric, decisions, and alignments, which in turn will likely have implications for regional security and for Turkey's EU accession prospects. Congressional positions could also influence Turkey's commitment to civilian-led, democratic government that enshrines individual, media, and minority rights; rule of law; and due process.

APPENDIX A. PROFILES OF KEY FIGURES IN TURKEY

Prime Minister Recep Tayyip Erdogan

Prime Minister Erdogan was born in Istanbul in 1954 and spent much of his childhood in his family's ancestral hometown of Rize on the Black Sea coast. He and his family returned to Istanbul for his teenage years, and he attended a religious *imam hatip* school. In the 1970s, Erdogan studied business at what is today Marmara University, played soccer semiprofessionally, and became politically active with the National Salvation Party, led by the pioneering Turkish Islamist figure (and eventual prime minister) Necmettin Erbakan. After the military banned all political parties in the wake of its 1980 coup, Erdogan became a business consultant and executive. When political life in Turkey resumed, Erdogan became a prominent local leader and organizer for Erbakan's new Welfare Party.

Erdogan was elected mayor of Istanbul in 1994 at the beginning of a wave of Islamist political victories in Turkey in the mid-1990s. He was removed from office, imprisoned for six months, and banned from parliamentary politics for religious incitement after he recited a poem in the southeastern city of Siirt in December 1997 that included the passage (translated from Turkish): "The mosques are our barracks, the domes our helmets, the minarets our bayonets and the faithful our soldiers."

After Erbakan's government resigned under military pressure in 1997 and the Welfare Party was disbanded, Erdogan became the founding chairman of the AKP in 2001. The AKP won a decisive electoral victory in 2002, securing the single-party rule that it has maintained since. After the election, a legal change allowed Erdogan to stand for parliament in a 2003 special election in Siirt, and after he won, Erdogan replaced Abdullah Gul as prime minister.

Erdogan and his personal popularity and charisma have been at the center of much of the domestic and foreign policy change that has occurred in Turkey in the past decade. In January 2009 at the World Economic Forum in Davos,

Switzerland, following the Gaza Strip conflict between Israel and Hamas, he left the panel discussion in which he was participating after perceiving a slight by the moderator (*Washington Post* columnist David Ignatius) and pointedly criticizing his fellow panelist Shimon Peres, president of Israel. His criticism of Israel and its actions has boosted his popularity at home and throughout the Muslim Middle East, where polls show that he may be the region's most popular world leader.

Erdogan is married and has two sons and two daughters. His wife Emine and daughters wear the headscarf. He is not fluent in English.

President Abdullah Gul

President Gul was born in 1950 in Kayseri in central Turkey. He studied economics in Turkey and England, and received his Ph.D. from Istanbul University, becoming a university professor and an economist at the Islamic Development Bank in Jeddah, Saudi Arabia. Gul was first elected to parliament from Kayseri in 1991 as a member of the Islamist Welfare Party, then, after it was disbanded, stayed on as a reform-minded member of the Islamist Virtue Party. Gul served on parliamentary assemblies of NATO and the Council of Europe. When the AKP was formed in 2001, he became deputy chairman and—briefly—its first prime minister after the successful election of 2002. When Erdogan took over the prime ministry in 2003, Gul became Turkey's foreign minister and helped accelerate Turkey's EU accession process. In 2007, the AKP nominated Gul for the presidency amid substantial secularist opposition, partly owing to statements from his early political career that indicated distaste for the secular nature of Turkey's republic. Parliament nevertheless elected Gul president. Many observers believe him to be a moderating influence on the Erdogan government. Gul is married with two sons and a daughter. His wife Hayrunissa and daughter wear the headscarf. He speaks fluent English.

Foreign Minister Ahmet Davutoglu

Foreign Minister Davutoglu was born in 1959 in Konya in central Turkey. He attended a German international school in Istanbul and received a Ph.D. in Political Science and International Relations from Bosphorus University. He became a university professor, spending time in Malaysia in the early 1990s before establishing himself as a scholar known for applying academic theory to practical matters of Turkish foreign policy and national security strategy. His book *Strategic Depth*, which was published in 2001 and has been translated into other languages but not English, is thought by some to represent a blueprint of sorts for the policies Davutoglu has since helped implement. Following the AKP's victory in 2002, Davutoglu was appointed chief foreign policy advisor to the prime minister. Upon his appointment as foreign minister in 2009, he quickly gained renown for articulating and applying his concepts of zero problems and strategic depth. He advocates for a preeminent role for Turkey in its surrounding region, but disputes the characterization of his policies by some observers as "neo-Ottomanism." He won an AKP parliamentary seat for the first time in June 2011. Davutoglu is married with four children. His wife Sare is a medical doctor. He speaks fluent English, as well as German and Arabic.

Opposition Leader Kemal Kilicdaroglu

Kilicdaroglu, the leader of the main opposition CHP, was born in 1948 in Tunceli province in eastern Turkey. After receiving an economics degree from what is now Gazi University in Ankara, Kilicdaroglu had a civil service career—first with the Finance Ministry, then as the director-general of the Social Security Organization. After retiring from the civil service, Kilicdaroglu became politically active with the CHP and was elected to parliament from Istanbul in 2002. He gained national prominence for his efforts to root out corruption among AKP officials and the AKP-affiliated mayor of Ankara. When CHP leader Deniz Baykal was forced to resign over a videotape sex scandal in May 2010, Kilicdaroglu was elected to replace him. In the first national election with him as party leader in June 2011, the CHP gained 23 seats in parliament, although not as many as some observers expected. Kilicdaroglu is married with a son and two daughters. He is an Alevi and speaks fluent French.

PKK Leader Abdullah Ocalan

Abdullah Ocalan was born in or around 1949 in southeastern Turkey (near Sanliurfa). After attending vocational high school in Ankara, Ocalan served in civil service posts in Diyarbakir and Istanbul until enrolling at Ankara

University in 1971. As his interest developed in socialism and Kurdish nationalism, Ocalan was jailed for seven months in 1972 for an illegal student demonstration. His time in prison with other activists helped inspire his political ambitions, and he became increasingly politically active upon his release. Ocalan founded the Marxist-Leninist-influenced PKK in 1978 and launched a separatist militant campaign against Turkish security forces—while also attacking the traditional Kurdish chieftain class—in 1984. He used Syrian territory as a safe haven. Syria forced Ocalan to leave in 1998 after Turkey threatened war for harboring him. After traveling to several different countries, Ocalan was captured in February 1999 in Kenya—possibly with U.S. help—and turned over to Turkish authorities. The PKK declared a cease-fire shortly thereafter. Ocalan was sentenced to death, in a trial later ruled unfair by the European Court of Human Rights, but when Turkey abolished the death penalty in 2002, the sentence was commuted to life imprisonment. He resides in a maximum-security prison on the island of Imrali in the Sea of Marmara, and was in solitary confinement until 2009.

Although acting PKK leader Murat Karayilan and other commanders have exercised direct control over PKK operations during Ocalan's imprisonment, some observers believe that Ocalan still ultimately controls the PKK through proxy communications. Although PKK violence resumed in 2003 and has since continued off-and-on, Ocalan has indicated that the organization is seeking a negotiated resolution that does not require forming a Kurdish state, and has reportedly engaged in talks with Turkish intelligence to that end.

Appendix B. List of Selected Turkish-Related Organizations in the United States

American Friends of Turkey (http://afot.us/)

American Research Institute in Turkey (http://ccat.sas.upenn.edu/ARIT/)

American Turkish Society (http://www.americanturkishsociety.org/)

American-Turkish Council (http://www.the-atc.org/)

Assembly of Turkish American Associations (http://www.ataa.org/)—component organizations from 17 states and District of Columbia

Ataturk Society of America (http://www.ataturksociety.org/)

Federation of Turkish American Associations

Institute of Turkish Studies (http://turkishstudies.org/)

SETA Foundation for Political, Economic and Social Research (http://setadc.org)

Turkic American Alliance (http://www.turkicamericanalliance.org/)

- West America Turkic Council (West region)—includes Pacifica Institute
- Turkish American Federation of Midwest (Midwest region)
- Turquoise Council of Americans and Eurasians (South region)—includes Institute of Interfaith Dialog
- Turkic American Federation of Southeast (Southeast region)—includes Istanbul Center
- Council of Turkic American Associations (Northeast region)
- Mid Atlantic Federation of Turkic American Associations (Mid-Atlantic region)—includes Rumi Forum

Turkish Coalition of America (http://www.tc-america.org/)

Turkish Confederation of Businessmen and Industrialists (TUSKON) (http://www.tuskonus.org/tuskon.php)

Turkish Cultural Foundation (http://www.turkishculturalfoundation.org/) Turkey Policy Center (http://www.turkishpolicycenter.com/)

Appendix C. Congressional Committee Reports of Armenian Genocide-Related Proposed Resolutions

Date Reported or of Vote for Report	Proposed Resolution(s)	Committee
April 5, 1984	S.J.Res. 87	Senate Judiciary
September 28, 1984	S.Res. 241	Senate Foreign Relations
July 9, 1985	H.J.Res. 192	House Post Office and Civil Service
July 23, 1987	H.J.Res. 132	House Post Office and Civil Service
August 3, 1987	H.Res. 238	House Rules
October 18, 1989	S.J.Res. 212	Senate Judiciary
October 11, 2000	H.Res. 596 and H.Res. 625	House Rules
October 10, 2007	H.Res. 106	House Foreign Affairs
March 4, 2010	H.Res. 252	House Foreign Affairs

End Notes

[1] Figure provided by officials of the Turkish Embassy to the United States, December 2011.

[2] Literacy rates in Turkey are higher than those of other large Muslim-majority countries. For example, the Central Intelligence Agency's World Factbook says that Egypt has a 71.4% total literacy rate, with only 59.4% of its women able to read and write, while Iran has a literacy rate of 77%, with 70.4% of women able to read and write.

[3] The youth population is considerably higher in Turkey than in countries in the EU, which Turkey aspires to join.

[4] The probability that information collected from the radar would be coordinated as necessary with another U.S. missile defense radar deployed in Israel has led to public statements of concern from Turkish officials and media, while some Members of Congress have insisted that sharing information for Israel's potential defense should be a condition of the radar's placement in Turkey. The text of a September 19, 2011, letter to President Barack Obama from six Senators on this subject is available at http://kirk.senate.gov/?p= press_release &id=299.

[5] "Balance of power," *Economist*, October 21, 2010.

[6] Gareth Jenkins, "Ergenekon, Sledgehammer, and the Politics of Turkish Justice: Conspiracies and Coincidences," *MERIA Journal*, vol. 15, no. 2, June 2011; Soli Ozel, "Military Resignations: Crisis or New Beginning?", German Marshall Fund of the United States, August 3, 2011.

[7] "Former Turkish armed forces chief ordered held for trial," *Reuters*, January 6, 2011.

[8] According to *Reuters*, an estimated one third of the AKP's parliamentary members in 2010, including Prime Minister Erdogan, attended *imam hatip* schools. Simon Akam, "A 'model' Islamic education from Turkey?", *Reuters*, February 23, 2010.

[9] AKP members generally use the acronym "AK Party" or "AK," partly because the Turkish word *ak* means "clean" and "unblemished," thus presenting an image of incorruptibility.

[10] For examples, see the U.S. State Department's Country Reports on Human Rights Practices 2010.

[11] During her July 2011 visit to Turkey, Secretary of State Hillary Clinton referred to these measures by saying, "I do not think it is necessary or in Turkey's interests to be cracking down. It seems to me inconsistent with all the other advances Turkey has made." "Clinton says Turkey must address concerns on backsliding on rights," *Associated Press*, July 16, 2011.

[12] Some of the penalties against the Dogan Group have been reversed on appeal to Turkish courts, while others remain under appeal.

[13] One widely discussed case involves the April 2011 arrest of Ahmet Sik and Nedem Sener, two prominent investigative journalists who were charged with involvement in the Ergenekon plots. Sik was reportedly close to finishing a book whose title translates as *The Imam's Army*. The book is reportedly about the Gulen movement's alleged infiltration of the Turkish police over the past 25 years. Several observers believe that the detentions of Sik and Sener were motivated by a desire to silence them rather than legitimate evidence of their criminal involvement. Jurgen Gottschlich, "Arrested Journalist's Book Claims Turkish Police Infiltrated by Islamic Movement," *Spiegel Online*, April 6, 2011.

[14] For example, Gulenists run *Zaman*, the most widely circulated newspaper in Turkey, and its English-language sister publication *Today's Zaman*.

[15] Gulen lives in seclusion at a retreat center with some of his adherents in Saylorsburg, PA, in the Pocono Mountains. He came to the United States in 1999 for medical treatment for a

cardiovascular condition, and elected to stay after an ultimately unsuccessful case was brought against him in Turkey charging that he sought to undermine Turkey's secular government.

[16] Gulen asserted in August 2010 that "we are still at an equal distance from every party. We never told anybody to enroll in a specific [party], attend its rallies or act as its supporters." "Gulen Endorses Reform Package, Appealing for 'Yes' on Sept. 12," *Today's Zaman*, August 1, 2010. He has backed AKP-proposed constitutional amendments, but distinguished his support for the substance of the initiatives from support for the party or individual leaders that had proposed them. "Gulen Says His Call for Yes Vote Not Linked to Political Motives," *Today's Zaman*, August 25, 2010.

[17] Days after the Al Qaeda terrorist attacks on September 11, 2011, Gulen took out advertisements in the *New York Times* and *Washington Post* condemning the attacks as incompatible with the teachings of Islam.

[18] Gulenists are involved with Turkish and Turkish-American trade associations and foundations active in the United States—both regionally and in the Washington, DC, area. Such organizations reportedly include the Turkic American Alliance umbrella of organizations and the business confederation TUSKON. Ilhan Tanir, "The Gulen movement plays big in Washington," *Hurriyet Daily News*, May 14, 2010; Helen Rose Ebaugh, *The Gulen Movement: A Sociological Analysis of a Civic Movement Rooted in Moderate Islam*, New York: Springer, 2010, p. 49. Gulenist organizations also have reportedly founded and operate more than 120 public charter schools in over 25 U.S. states. These schools have generated publicity both for their high academic quality and for questions and possible federal investigations regarding their hiring and business practices. Stephanie Saul, "Charter Schools Tied to Turkey Grow in Texas," *New York Times*, June 6, 2011; Martha Woodall and Claudio Gatti, "U.S. charter-school network with Turkish link draws federal attention," *Philadelphia Inquirer*, March 20, 2011.

[19] Turkish Economic Ministry correspondence with CRS, December 2011.

[20] OECD Economic Outlook No. 86, November 2009.

[21] "TEXT-Fitch revises Turkey's outlook to stable," *Reuters*, November 23, 2011.

[22] Gokhan Bacik, "Envisioning the Asia-Pacific Century: Turkey between the United States and China," *On Turkey*, German Marshall Fund of the United States, December 8, 2011.

[23] Transatlantic Academy, *Getting to Zero: Turkey, Its Neighbors, and the West*, June 2010, citing Turkish government statistics.

[24] In Footnote 2 of a September 2011 report, the International Crisis Group stated that Turkish government figures estimate that 11,700 Turks have been killed since fighting began in the early 1980s. This figure includes Turkish security personnel of various types and Turkish civilians (including Turkish Kurds who are judged not to have been PKK combatants). The same report states that Turkish estimates of PKK dead during the same time period run from 30,000 to 40,000. International Crisis Group, Turkey: Ending the PKK Insurgency, Europe Report No. 213, September 20, 2011.

[25] U.S. Treasury Department Press Release, "Five PKK Leaders Designated Narcotics Traffickers," April 20, 2011.

[26] In the 2011 election, 61 members of the Kurdish nationalist Peace and Democracy Party (BDP) ran as independents for individual geographic constituencies because of a calculation that the party would not reach the 10% threshold. These independents won 36 of the constituencies and 6% of the national vote.

[27] For information comparing and contrasting Sunnism and Shiism, see CRS Report RS21745, *Islam: Sunnis and Shiites*, by Christopher M. Blanchard; and CRS Report WVB00001, *Sunni and Shi'a Islam: Video Brief*, by Christopher M. Blanchard.

[28] Ayla Albayrak, "Turkey's Erdogan Promises Probe of Airstrike," *wsj.com*, December 30, 2011.

[29] Emiliano Alessandri, "Democratization and Europeanization in Turkey After the September 12 Referendum," *Insight Turkey*, vol. 12, no. 4, fall 2010.

[30] The U.S. Commission on International Religious Freedom has included Turkey on its watch list since 2009. The commission's website carries its 2011 annual report (covering April 2010-March 2011). See also the State Department's International Religious Freedom Report for July-December 2010, September 13, 2011.

[31] The Patriarchate traces its roots to the Apostle Andrew. The most commonly articulated congressional grievances on behalf of the Patriarchate—whose ecumenicity is not acknowledged by the Turkish government, but also not objected to when acknowledged by others—are the non-operation of the Halki Theological School on Heybeliada Island near Istanbul, the requirement that the Patriarch be a Turkish citizen, and the failure of the Turkish government to return previously confiscated properties.

[32] H.Res. 306 was sponsored by Representative Edward Royce. Other proposed resolutions from the 112th Congress include H.Res. 180 ("Urging Turkey to respect the rights and religious freedoms of the Ecumenical Patriarchate"), and S.Res. 196 ("A resolution calling upon the Government of Turkey to facilitate the reopening of the Ecumenical Patriarchate's Theological School of Halki without condition or further delay").

[33] According to reports, the foundations would receive compensation for property since transferred to third parties. See Sebnum Arsu, "Turkish Government to Return Seized Property to Religious Minorities," *New York Times*, August 29, 2011.

[34] Dorian Jones, "Turkey: Making Room for Religious Minorities," *EurasiaNet.org*, October 3, 2011.

[35] CRS correspondence with U.S. diplomat based in Turkey, November 2011.

[36] For a critique of viewpoints that favor a Turkey-like military-led transition in Egypt, see Steven Cook, "The Turkish Model for Egypt? Beware of False Analogies," *blogs.cfr.org*, February 4, 2011.

[37] Nathalie Tocci, Omer Taspinar, Henri Barkey, Eduard Soler i Lecha, and Hassan Nafaa, *Turkey and the Arab Spring: Implications for Turkish Foreign Policy from a Transatlantic Perspective*, German Marshall Fund of the United States, 2011; Sinan Ulgen, *From Inspiration to Aspiration: Turkey in the New Middle East*, Carnegie Europe, December 2011.

[38] Saban Kardas, "Quest for Strategic Autonomy Continues, or How to Make Sense of Turkey's 'New Wave,'" *On Turkey* Analysis, German Marshall Fund of United States, November 28, 2011.

[39] Hugh Pope and Peter Harling, "Are there 'zero problems' for Turkey?", *Daily Star* (Lebanon), November 29, 2011. See also Steven Cook, "Turkey: From Zero Problems to Cok Problems," *blogs.cfr.org*, November 14, 2011.

[40] The deaths took place under disputed circumstances.

[41] The report is available at http://go.ynet.co.il/pic/news/Palmer-Committee-Final-report.pdf. The panel was chaired by former New Zealand Prime Minister Sir Geoffrey Palmer, and included former Colombian President Alvaro Uribe and one participant each from Turkey and Israel. The report expressly provided that its findings were not intended to decide legal questions. Upon the report's leak, Turkish officials disputed the report's finding that Israel's

naval blockade of the Gaza Strip was legal, notwithstanding the report's criticism of Israel's handling of the incident itself.

[42] Turkey similarly downgraded diplomatic relations with Israel in 1980 following Israel's enactment of a law on the status of Jerusalem that was deemed a violation of international law by U.N. Security Council Resolution 478. Resolution 478 passed on August 20, 1980 by a vote of 14-0, with the United States as the lone abstention. Turkey reinstated Israel's ambassador in 1992 following the 1991 Madrid Conference that signaled the beginning of the Middle East peace process. Linda Gradstein, "No end in sight for downward spiral in Turkish-Israeli ties," *JTA*, September 6, 2011.

[43] *Time* magazine staff interview with Turkish Prime Minister Recep Tayyip Erdogan, *globalspin.blogs.time.com*, September 26, 2011.

[44] Transcript of remarks by Secretary Panetta at Saban Forum, Brookings Institution, Washington, DC, December 2, 2011, available at http://www.defense.gov/transcripts /transcript.aspx?transcriptid=4937.

[45] "Turkey-Israel fallout threatens wider damage, say analysts," *Agence France Presse*, September 2, 2011.

[46] In the House, Representative Dina Titus sponsored H.Res. 1532, which was not passed but garnered 23 co-sponsors. H.Res. 1532 would have called upon the Secretary of State to investigate the "role of any foreign governments, including the Republic of Turkey, which may have aided and abetted the organizers of the recent Gaza Flotilla mission to breach Israeli coastal security and assault the naval defense forces of the State of Israel."

[47] James Traub, "Turkey's Rules," *New York Times Magazine*, January 20, 2011.

[48] For more information, see CRS Report RL33487, *Unrest in Syria and U.S. Sanctions Against the Asad Regime*, by Jeremy M. Sharp and Christopher M. Blanchard.

[49] The initial sanctions announced included: (1) suspending the Turkey-Syria High Level Strategic Cooperation Council; (2) travel ban and asset freeze on leading regime officials and businessmen believed to be responsible for or supportive of violent repression of protests; (3) embargo on sales of weapons and military equipment; (4) preventing the transit of weapons/military equipment to Syria from third countries through Turkey; (5) halting dealings with Syria's central bank; (6) freezing financial assets of Syrian government in Turkey; (7) halting lending relationships with Syrian government; (8) prohibiting new transactions with Syrian Trade Bank; and (9) suspending the Eximbank credit agreement, which had been intended for financing infrastructure projects in Syria. After Syria retaliated in December 2011 with its own sanctions, including suspending the Turkey-Syria free trade agreement and imposing a tariff (about 30%) and duties on Turkish imports, Turkey responded with a similar tariff on Syrian imports.

[50] Ipek Yezdani, "More Syrian refugees come to Hatay camps," *Hurriyet Daily News*, January 7, 2012.

[51] See, e.g., Samia Nakhoul, "Analysis: Turkey and allies want Syria's Assad out, just not yet," *Reuters*, December 16, 2011; Phil Sands, "Assad: friend or foe of the Kurds?", *The National* (United Arab Emirates), January 4, 2012.

[52] The proposed elements of the European Phased Adaptive Approach to missile defense proposed by the Obama Administration and a deployment timeline are described in a September 17, 2009, White House press release available at http://www.whitehouse.gov /the_press_office/FACT-SHEET-US-Missile-Defense-Policy-A-Phased-
Adaptive-Approach-for-Missile-Defense-in-Europe/ See also CRS Report R41549, Missile Defense and NATO's Lisbon Summit, by Steven A. Hildreth and Carl Ek.

[53] Thom Shanker, "U.S. Hails Deal with Turkey on Missile Shield," *New York Times*, September 15, 2011.

[54] "Part of NATO missile defense system goes live in Turkey," *CNN*, January 16, 2012.

[55] Per section 1245 of P.L. 112-81, these sanctions do not apply to a financial institution if the President determines and reports to Congress that the institution's primary country of jurisdiction has significantly reduced oil imports from Iran, or if the President waives the sanctions for national security reasons.

[56] Taylan Bilgic, "Iran sanctions bode ill for Turkey's economy," *Hurriyet Daily News*, January 6, 2012.

[57] For further information, see CRS Report R41761, *Turkey-U.S. Defense Cooperation: Prospects and Challenges*, by Jim Zanotti.

[58] "US deployed Predators to Incirlik: Davutoglu," *Hurriyet Daily News*, November 13, 2011. According to Secretary of Defense Panetta, the Iraqi government has given the United States permission to keep flying Predator drones on surveillance missions over northern Iraq. Craig Whitlock, "U.S. drones allowed in Iraqi skies," washingtonpost.com/ blogs/checkpoint-washington, December 16, 2011.

[59] "Procurement, Turkey," *Jane's Sentinel Security Assessment - Eastern Mediterranean*, December 16, 2010; "US-Turkey agree on delivery schedule for Predators," *Today's Zaman*, September 25, 2011.

[60] For more information on this subject, see CRS Report R41136, *Cyprus: Reunification Proving Elusive*, by Vincent Morelli.

[61] Turkey views its protective role as justified given its status as one of the three guaranteeing powers of the 1960 Treaty of Guarantee that was signed at the time Cyprus gained its independence. The United Kingdom and Greece are the other two guarantors.

[62] Turkish intervention in Cyprus with U.S.-supplied arms prompted Congress to impose an embargo on military assistance and arms sales to Turkey from 1975 to 1978. This Cold War-era disruption in U.S.-Turkey relations is often cited by analysts as a major factor in Turkey's continuing efforts to avoid overdependence on the United States or any other country for military equipment or expertise.

[63] Turkey retains between 30,000 and 40,000 troops on the island (supplemented by approximately 5,000 Turkish Cypriot soldiers and 26,000 reserves). "Turkish Republic of Northern Cyprus," *Jane's Sentinel Security Assessment - Eastern Mediterranean*, October 30, 2009. This is countered by a Greek Cypriot force of approximately 12,000 (including roughly 1,300 Greek officers and soldiers seconded to Cyprus) with reported access to 50,000 reserves. "Cyprus," *Jane's World Armies*, November 3, 2011. The United Nations maintains a peacekeeping mission (UNFICYP) of approximately 900 personnel within a buffer zone headquartered in Cyprus's divided capital of Nicosia. Since the mission's inception in 1964, UNFICYP has suffered 179 fatalities. The United Kingdom maintains approximately 3,000 personnel at two sovereign military bases on the southern portion of the island at Akrotiri and Dhekelia.

[64] "Gas drilling heightens east Mediterranean tension," *UPI*, September 16, 2011.

[65] CRS conversation with Turkish think tank analyst in Istanbul, September 30, 2011.

[66] For more information, see CRS Report RL33453, *Armenia, Azerbaijan, and Georgia: Political Developments and Implications for U.S. Interests*, by Jim Nichol.

[67] Nagorno-Karabakh is a predominantly ethnic-Armenian-populated enclave within Azerbaijan's international borders. Disputes over its status led to armed conflict in 1991 in parallel with the Soviet Union's dissolution and the independence of both Armenia and Azerbaijan. The conflict ended with a 1994 ceasefire, but Armenian troops still occupy portions of the

territory. The Minsk Group of the Organization for Security and Cooperation in Europe (co-chaired by the United States, Russia, and France, and including both Armenia and Azerbaijan as well as Turkey and a number of other European countries) has been trying to negotiate a permanent settlement since then.

[68] In the meantime, Turkey and Azerbaijan signed a 10-year security and mutual assistance agreement in August 2010.

[69] Serkan Demirtas, "Turkey examines ways to revive Armenia dialogue," *Hurriyet Daily News*, December 7, 2011.

[70] Information dated January 2011 provided to CRS by Turkish Embassy in Washington, DC.

[71] This subsection was co-authored with Michael Ratner, Specialist in Energy Policy.

[72] The U.S. energy strategy in Europe is designed to work together with European nations and the European Union to seek ways to diversify Europe's energy supplies. The focus of U.S. efforts has been on establishing a southern corridor route for Central Asian and Middle Eastern natural gas supplies to be shipped to Europe. Turkey factors into the proposed pipeline projects to transport natural gas from the Caspian and the Middle East to Europe in an effort to diversify European natural gas sources. See, e.g., Transatlantic Academy, *Getting to Zero: Turkey, Its Neighbors, and the West*, June 2010.

[73] Suzanne Gusten, "Forging Ahead on Nuclear Energy in Turkey," *New York Times*, March 23, 2011.

[74] Turkey is also a signatory to the Nuclear Non-Proliferation Treaty (NPT) and has a safeguards agreement and additional protocol in place with the International Atomic Energy Agency (IAEA). It is an observer to—not a full participant in—the International Framework for Nuclear Energy Cooperation (IFNEC, formerly known as the Global Nuclear Energy Partnership) founded by the United States, Russia, China, France, and Japan in 2007. IFNEC promotes the peaceful use of nuclear energy by helping establish reprocessing centers for nuclear fuel.

[75] See World Nuclear Association website, "Nuclear Power in Turkey," updated December 2011.

[76] Adam P. Williams, "Amid Growing Hopes for the Future, Turkish Nuclear Energy Ambitions Suffer Setback," *WMD Insights*, December 2008/January 2009. Turkey is one of the regional countries analysts routinely mention could decide to pursue its own nuclear weapons program in the event that one or more countries in the region, such as Iran, achieves or declares a nuclear weapons capability. Israel is generally believed by most analysts to have had a nuclear arsenal since the late 1960s, but it maintains a policy of "nuclear opacity" wherein its nuclear weapons status remains officially undeclared. For discussion of Turkey and nuclear weapons, see CRS Report R41761, *Turkey-U.S. Defense Cooperation: Prospects and Challenges*, by Jim Zanotti.

[77] For more information on this subject, see CRS Report RS22517, *European Union Enlargement: A Status Report on Turkey's Accession Negotiations*, by Vincent Morelli.

[78] Dan Bilefsky, "For Turkey, Lure of Tie to Europe Is Fading," *New York Times*, December 4, 2011. According to the *Transatlantic Trends* surveys of the German Marshall Fund of the United States, the percentage of Turks who think that Turkish EU membership would be a good thing was 73% in 2004 and 48% in 2011.

[79] Turkey's unwillingness to open its ports to Greek Cypriot trade according to the Additional Protocol that it signed at the outset of the accession process in 2005 has prompted the EU Council to block eight out of the 35 chapters of the *acquis communautaire* that Turkey would be required to meet to the Council's satisfaction in order to gain EU membership. Thus far, one of the chapters has been fully negotiated, and 13 others have been opened.

[80] European Commission Staff Working Paper, Turkey 2011 Progress Report, October 12, 2011.

[81] See http://ec.europa.eu/enlargement/candidate-countries/turkey/financial-assistance /index_en.htm for further information.

[82] See, e.g., Hajrudin Somun, "Turkish Foreign Policy in the Balkans and 'Neo-Ottomanism': A Personal Account," *Insight Turkey*, vol. 13, no. 3, summer 2011; Yigal Schleifer, "Turkey's Neo-Ottoman Problem," *World Politics Review*, February 16, 2010; Greg Bruno, "Turkey's Near Abroad," Council on Foreign Relations Analysis Brief, September 19, 2008.

[83] See Gareth Jenkins, "On the edge – The AKP shifts Turkey's political compass," *Jane's Intelligence Review*, August 2, 2010.

[84] "US official: Turkey must demonstrate commitment to West," *Today's Zaman*, June 28, 2010.

[85] Ercan Yavuz, "Israeli-caused instability makes its way to Turkey's security document," *Today's Zaman*, October 29, 2010.

[86] For example, during a September 2011 trip to Libya, Erdogan criticized what he perceived to be Britain's and France's overly commercial interests in the country—despite Turkey's own well-documented commercial interests in Libya and participation in and support for the 2011 NATO operation there.

[87] Carol Migdalovitz, "AKP's Domestically Driven Foreign Policy," *Turkish Policy Quarterly*, vol. 9, no. 4, spring 2011.

[88] Sevil Kucukkosum, "Turks see U.S. as biggest external threat, poll results show," *Hurriyet Daily News & Economic Review*, January 5, 2011. A December 2010 poll, taken by the MetroPOLL Strategic and Social Research Center, which is affiliated with Turkey's ruling Justice and Development Party (AKP), stated that 43% of respondents viewed the United States as Turkey's primary external threat, with Israel in second place with 24%. Iran was a distant third with 3%. Reports posit that the 2003 U.S.-led invasion of Iraq is a major shaper of the Turkish people's threat perception, along with U.S. closeness to Israel and congressional action on Armenia. Ibid.

[89] British Broadcasting Corporation World Service Poll, "Views of US Continue to Improve in 2011 BBC Country Rating Poll," March 7, 2011. The BBC poll, which was conducted from December 2010 to February 2011, claimed that 35% of Turks believe that U.S. influence in the world is positive (up from 13% in 2010), and that 49% believe that U.S. influence is negative (down from 68% in 2010).

[90] For detailed information on this subject, see CRS Report R41761, *Turkey-U.S. Defense Cooperation: Prospects and Challenges*, by Jim Zanotti.

[91] Henri J. Barkey, "Turkey's New Global Role," Carnegie Endowment for International Peace, November 17, 2010. The challenge for U.S. officials to manage cooperation with Turkey could be magnified by the way the U.S. government is structured to work with Turkey. Former U.S. ambassador to Turkey Mark Parris has said, "For reasons of self-definition and Cold War logic, Turkey is considered a European nation. It is therefore assigned, for purposes of policy development and implementation, to the subdivisions responsible for Europe: the European Bureau (EUR) at the State Department; the European Command (EUCOM) at the Pentagon; the Directorate for Europe at the [National Security Council (NSC)], etc. Since the end of the Cold War, however, and progressively since the 1990-91 Gulf War and 9/11, the most serious issues in U.S.-Turkish relations – and virtually all of the controversial ones – have arisen in areas outside "Europe." The majority, in fact, stem from developments in areas which in Washington are the responsibility of offices dealing with the Middle East: the Bureau for Near East Affairs (NEA) at State; Central Command (CENTCOM) at the Pentagon; the Near East and South Asia Directorate at NSC." Omer Taspinar, "The Rise of Turkish Gaullism: Getting Turkish-American Relations Right,"

Insight Turkey, vol. 13, no. 1, winter 2011, quoting an unpublished 2008 paper by Mark Parris.

[92] Joshua W. Walker, "U.S.-Turkish Relations: Modesty and Revitalization," *On Turkey*, German Marshall Fund of the United States, December 15, 2011.

[93] "Procurement, Turkey," *Jane's Sentinel Security Assessment - Eastern Mediterranean*, December 16, 2010. Previous potential sales of Reapers to NATO allies such as the United Kingdom, Germany, and Italy were notified to Congress in 2008 and 2009 with the understanding that the drones would be used to support coalition operations in Iraq and Afghanistan.

[94] "US-Turkey agree on delivery schedule for Predators," *Today's Zaman*, September 25, 2011.

[95] "U.S. Vows to Support Turkey over Kurdish Rebels," *Agence France Presse*, December 18, 2011.

[96] Craig Whitlock, "Pentagon agrees to sell three attack helicopters to Turkey," *Washington Post*, November 1, 2011.

[97] "US deployed Predators to Incirlik: Davutoglu," *Hurriyet Daily News*, November 13, 2011.

[98] Robert Tait and Ewen McCaskill, "Turkey threatens 'serious consequences' after US vote on Armenian genocide," *Guardian* (UK), March 5, 2010.

[99] The EU states recognizing a genocide are France, Germany, Italy, Sweden, Belgium, the Netherlands, Lithuania, Poland, Slovakia, Greece, and Cyprus. The European Parliament has also recognized the deaths as genocide.

[100] Scott Sayare and Sebnem Arsu, "Turkey Lashes Out Over Bill About French Genocide," *New York Times*, December 23, 2011. Switzerland and Slovenia have previously criminalized denial of an Armenian genocide.

[101] CRS correspondence with Department of Commerce official, December 2011.

[102] For more detailed information on bilateral efforts to promote trade, see U.S. Department of Commerce Fact Sheet: U.S.-Turkey Framework for Strategic Economic and Commercial Cooperation, October 14, 2010.

[103] CRS conversation with representative of Turkish business association, December 2011.

[104] Given Turkey's customs union with the EU, a full free trade agreement between the United States and Turkey would not be possible without a U.S.-EU free trade agreement.

[105] In December 2011, the *New York Times* profiled Turkey as an attractive destination for foreign capital given its growing consumer market and relative political and financial stability. Mark Scott, "In Turkey, Western Companies Find Stability and Growth," *New York Times*, December 23, 2011.

[106] Information provided to CRS by Turkish Ministry of Economy, September 2011.

In: Turkey and the U.S.
Editors: S. N. Boothe and R. Hickman
ISBN: 978-1- 62081-276-1

Chapter 2

TURKEY-UNITED STATES DEFENSE COOPERATION: PROSPECTS AND CHALLENGES*

Jim Zanotti

SUMMARY

Congress and the Obama Administration are seeking to manage longstanding bilateral and North Atlantic Treaty Organization (NATO)-based defense cooperation with Turkey at a time when a more independent Turkish foreign policy course and changes in regional security conditions are creating new challenges for both countries. Defense cooperation rooted in shared threat perceptions from the Cold War era and built on close U.S. ties with the Turkish military leadership now must be reconciled with a decline of the military's political influence in Turkish society and some negative turns in Turkish popular sentiment toward the United States over the past decade. At the same time, Turkey's importance as a U.S. ally has arguably increased on issues of global significance in its surrounding region that include Iraq, Iran, Afghanistan, and the Israeli-Palestinian peace process. In early 2011, Turkey's regional role has arguably become even more prominent—exemplified by its significant involvement politically and militarily on the question of NATO's intervention in Libya.

---

* This is an edited, reformatted and augmented version of Congressional Research Service, Publication No. R41761, dated April 8, 2011.

How Congress and the Administration manage defense cooperation with Turkey in this evolving context is likely to have a significant bearing on U.S. national security interests, as well as on both U.S. and Turkish calculations of the mutual benefits and leverage involved in the cooperative relationship. Some officials and analysts believe that, in at least some respects, the United States needs Turkey more than Turkey needs the United States. Others counter that claims of Turkish leverage over the United States are exaggerated.

Possible general congressional and Administration approaches to U.S.-Turkey defense cooperation ("Possible U.S. Policy Approaches") include

- avoiding major recharacterizations of the alliance, while emphasizing and expressing confidence that existing NATO and bilateral relationships—with their long legacies—can address mutual security challenges;
- according high priority to the alliance and revising expectations for it by accommodating new developments within and outside of Turkey;
- linking cooperation in some way to Turkey's relations with certain third-party countries or non-state actors—including Iran, Israel, Hamas, Armenia, and China—or to Turkish actions on issues of U.S. national security interest; and
- using or combining any of these approaches on a case-by-case basis.

Specific issues that remain of significant importance for Congress (see "Specific Issues and Possible Options for Congress"), given its authority to appropriate funds, review major arms sales, consider non-binding resolutions, and provide general oversight include the following:

- *Continued military access to Turkish bases and transport corridors*: The ongoing availability to the United States and NATO of Turkish bases and transport corridors—which have been used heavily for military operations in Iraq, Afghanistan, and Libya—is valuable and remains a possible point of contention and leverage. The extent of its importance and of alternatives may be subject to further analysis.
- *Future of Turkey-Israel relations*: U.S. efforts to maintain alliances with both Turkey and Israel could be made more complicated if relations between them do not improve—potentially influencing the regional security environment.
- *Missile defense radar*: Whether Turkey agrees in 2011 to host a U.S. forward-deployed radar for missile defense as part of the

NATO system may depend on its perceptions of whether doing so would be more likely to cultivate stability or to be unduly provocative to neighboring countries.

- *Arms sales and industrial cooperation*: Turkey continues to seek advanced military equipment from U.S. sources, particularly with respect to fighter and drone aircraft, helicopters, and missile defense systems (see "Arms Sales and Industrial Cooperation"). At the same time, Turkey is increasingly diversifying its defense contacts and procurement relationships with non-NATO countries.
- *Military and security assistance*: Although the United States no longer provides major annual grant aid to Turkey's military, assistance continues to foster cooperation on counterterrorism, law enforcement, and military training and education.

INTRODUCTION: ISSUES FOR CONGRESS

The United States enjoys a strong legacy of defense cooperation with Turkey, both bilaterally and in the North Atlantic Treaty Organization (NATO), dating from the onset of the Cold War. For both countries, mutual cooperation has major implications for national security priorities in Turkey's surrounding region—particularly the greater Middle East. A more independent Turkish foreign policy course—reflected in recent international events involving Iran, Israel, and other countries—has raised concerns among some Members of Congress.

This, coupled with a decline of the military's influence in Turkish society, may affect prospects and present challenges for bilateral and NATO defense cooperation, while also generating ongoing debate over which country needs the other more to pursue and achieve its national security objectives.

A challenge for U.S. officials—particularly in the White House, the Defense Department (DOD; both civilian and military branches), and the State Department—is to adjust future modes of bilateral interaction with Turkey on defense matters to account for greater fluidity within the internal Turkish civil-military power structure.

Determining proper interlocutors for both countries on different but interrelated questions of (1) grand strategy (which involves political objectives beyond pure military matters), (2) military strategy, and (3) tactical and operational objectives could lead to an approach that is more multidimensional than the well-established pattern some observers see in which the State Department and other U.S. officials rely on the "Pentagon to wield its influence."[1]

Areas of potential interest or concern for Congress, as well as other U.S. policymakers, include the following:

- *Overall Defense Relationship*: Reconciling regional perceptions of growing Turkish influence and declining U.S. influence with persisting Turkish interest in defense cooperation to address immediate security and deterrence needs.
- *NATO/Missile Defense*: Turkey's role in NATO, both in
  (1) defining the scope of alliance action and objectives in possible cases of intervention, such as Libya; and
  (2) regarding aspects of alliance-wide defense, such as an approved missile defense system that could feature a radar station and other elements in Turkey to counter threats from Iran and elsewhere.
- *Iraq and Afghanistan*: Cooperating with Turkey to achieve stability and a reduced threat of terrorism from Iraq and Afghanistan through
  (1) joint counterterrorism efforts,
  (2) use of Turkish bases and territory for cargo transport,
  (3) possible arms sales, and
  (4) direct involvement of Turkish non-combat troops (in Afghanistan) and trainers.
- *Israel*: Addressing implications of increasingly distant Turkey-Israel relations on U.S.-Turkey defense cooperation.
- *Armenian Genocide Resolution*: Continuing defense cooperation with Turkey in light of a possible adverse Turkish reaction to a potential U.S. congressional resolution or presidential statement characterizing World War I-era actions of the Ottoman Empire against Armenians as genocide. Expectations regarding the likely nature and extent of a possible adverse Turkish reaction vary.[2]
- *Future Prospects for Various Modes of Defense Cooperation*: These include
  (1) joint exercises and missions;
  (2) stationing of U.S./NATO personnel and arms (including a reported nuclear weapons arsenal) in Turkey;
  (3) forms of defense-related U.S. aid, including International Military Education and Training; and
  (4) defense industrial cooperation.

Overview of Cooperation

Background

Turkey's NATO accession in 1952 during the early years of the Cold War was premised upon the concept of a "mutuality of benefits." Turkey received U.S. security guarantees against Soviet aggression. In return, the United States and its other Western allies could (1) station and base troops and equipment in Turkey for defensive and intelligence-gathering purposes, (2) count on Turkish control over Soviet access to the Mediterranean through the Bosporus and Dardanelles straits and on Turkish co-belligerency in case of an attack, and (3) contain Turkish-Greek tensions within the NATO umbrella.

Although events over the last few years have strained U.S.-Turkey defense cooperation to some extent, tension in the bilateral relationship is not new. According to one scholar, "Apart from a honeymoon in the early 1950s, the US-Turkish alliance has always been troubled."[3] Turkey's relations with Greece and its involvement in Cyprus have been the focus of many of these troubles. When in 1974 Turkey sent troops using U.S.-supplied arms to intervene on behalf of the Turkish Cypriot minority, Congress responded by placing an embargo on U.S. military grants and arms sales to Turkey that lasted from 1975 until 1978,[4] despite objections voiced by the executive branch.

The embargo delivered a serious blow to the Turkish military's operational readiness. Turkey, in turn, closed U.S. defense and intelligence installations on Turkish territory throughout the period of the embargo (except for those installations that had a purely NATO function). In addition, according to a 2005 article in the journal *Turkish Studies*, "The resentment and loss of confidence in the US transformed the alliance to a great extent and made Turkey focus on two important strategic priorities from then onwards: to diversify the sources of arms imports and to improve the development of a domestic arms industry."[5]

Yet, some believe that the nature and degree of U.S.-Turkey tensions, and how they affect mutual threat perceptions and defense priorities, might be changing. Longtime Turkey analyst Henri Barkey of the Carnegie Endowment of International Peace wrote in 2010 that "Turkish-American relations were always difficult and acrimonious even in the best of times.... What is different now is that the issues over which Turkey and America differ are far more numerous and complicated than in the past."[6] The vote of the Turkish Grand National Assembly (Parliament) in 2003 not to allow U.S. troops to use

Turkey's border with Iraq as a second front in their invasion of the country showed the United States that in its defense relationship with Turkey, it could no longer rely solely on past legacies of cooperation and its close ties with the Turkish military.

The onset of more numerous and complicated differences within the U.S.-Turkey alliance may be reflected in Turkish popular sentiment toward the United States. Results from a December 2010 poll stated that despite the long-time alliance, and despite several potential threats along Turkey's borders, the Turkish people see the United States as its biggest external threat by a wide margin.[7] This apparent sentiment exists within a context of Turks' generally low favorability ratings for foreign countries, partly based on historical concerns about encirclement by outside powers— particularly the West and Russia. Reports posit that the 2003 U.S.-led invasion of Iraq is a major shaper of the Turkish people's threat perception,[8] along with U.S. closeness to Israel and congressional action on Armenia.[9] However, a British Broadcasting Corporation (BBC) poll released in March 2011 indicates that—though still negative on balance—Turkish perceptions of U.S. influence in the world have improved significantly from a year earlier.[10] Future trends in these perceptions are likely to influence democratically elected Turkish leaders' approaches to strategic cooperation.

Since 1948, the United States has provided Turkey with approximately $13.8 billion in overall military assistance—$8.2 billion in monetary and in-kind grants and $5.6 billion in loans. However, the end of the Cold War and Turkey's increasing economic and military self-sufficiency led to the discontinuance of most aid. Current annual military and security assistance is limited to International Military Education and Training (IMET); International Narcotics Control and Law Enforcement (INCLE); and Non-proliferation, Antiterrorism, Demining and Related Programs (NADR) funds. For a more detailed breakdown of this assistance, see Table 1 below; and for a historical overview and chronology of U.S.-Turkey defense cooperation, see Appendix A.

Turkey's Importance to U.S. National Security

Arguably, Turkey is a more significant ally for the United States at present than during the Cold War. With several challenges to U.S. national security emanating from the greater Middle East, the United States has already shown that it seeks to use Turkey's geographic location for its advantage, and it is likely that future U.S. regional interests will dictate a similar U.S. outlook. Given Turkey's location near several global hotspots, the availability of its territory for the stationing and transport of arms, cargo, and personnel remains valuable for the United States and NATO (see Figure 1 and "Bases and Transport Corridors" below). In addition, Turkey, with its sizeable armed forces and modern weapons systems, is considered to be among the strongest military powers in its region, and continuing Turkish economic growth and increases in domestic military spending and arms exports support the view that it will play a major role in regional security for years to come.[11] As Turkey's regional influence expands through economic, political, and cultural means, its importance has arguably increased for the United States on issues of global significance that include Iraq, Iran, Afghanistan, and Israeli-Palestinian issues.

Table 1. U.S. Military and Security Assistance to Turkey (historical $ in millions)

Fiscal Year(s)	Foreign Mil. Fin.	Excess Defense Articles	Int'l Mil. Ed. and Training	NADR	INCLE	Other Grants	Total Grants	Loans
1948-1975	—	869.0	111.8	—	—	3,406.0	4,386.8	185.0
1976-1981	—	—	3.4	—	1.0	10.5	14.9	952.9
1982-1992	1,884.0	—	36.4	—	6.7	1,362.1	3,289.2	2,769.1
1993-2001	—	205.1	14.0	0.1	3.2	—	222.4	1,678.1
2002-2008	170.0	21.1	23.7	8.6	0.1	—	223.5	—
2009	1.0	—	3.2	1.9	0.5	—	6.6	—
2010	—	—	5.0	3.0	—	—	8.0	—
2011 Request	—	—	4.0	1.4	0.5	—	5.9	—
2012 Request	—	—	4.0	—	0.5	—	4.5	—
TOTAL	2,055.0	1,095.2	205.5	14.0	12.5	4,778.6	8,160.8	5,585.1

Source: U.S. Agency for International Development, U.S. State Department.

Notes: All amounts are approximate. NADR stands for Nonproliferation, Antiterrorism, Demining and Related Programs; INCLE stands for International Narcotics Control and Law Enforcement.

In early 2011, Turkey's regional role has arguably become even more prominent—exemplified by its significant involvement politically and militarily on the question of NATO's intervention in Libya—as political change and unrest generates international debate about links between internal governance, humanitarian and civil society issues, and regional security. Moreover, Turkey's growing importance as a regional energy transport hub whose supply sources are not limited to (even though they include) Russia and

Iran elevates the continued importance of Turkey's security for world energy markets.[12]

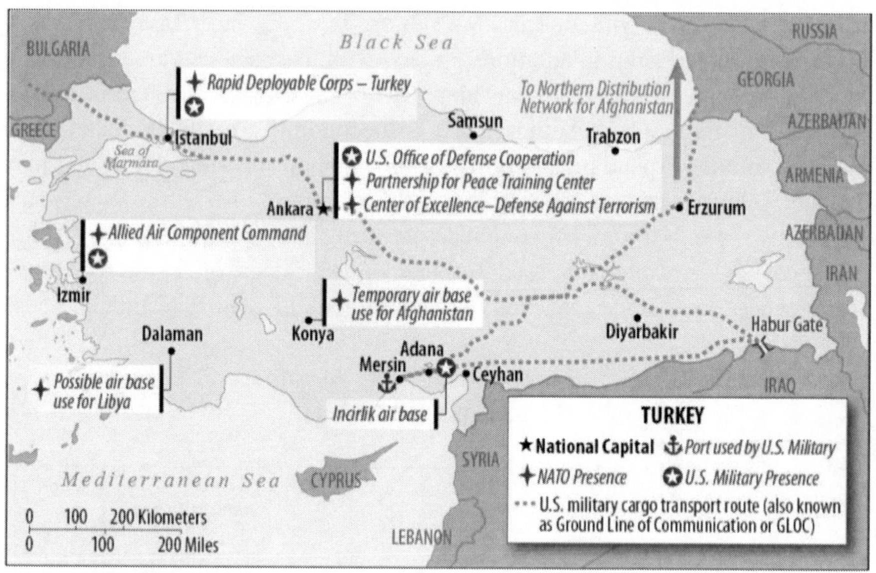

Source: DOD; NATO.

Notes: All locations are approximate. Incirlik air base is a Turkish base, part of which is used for limited purposes by the U.S. military.

Figure 1. Map of U.S. and NATO Military Presence and Transport Routes in Turkey.

This affects both U.S. and Turkish calculations of the mutual benefits and leverage of defense cooperation. The United States hopes that involving Turkey's military and territory in various defense initiatives (such as in Libya and Afghanistan, and with NATO missile defense) both provides greater influence for the United States with regional actors and politically legitimizes U.S. actions to Muslim populations. Turkish leaders use the importance the United States confers upon Turkey's role both to seek benefits from the United States and to elevate their prestige in dealings with other countries. At the same time, however, many high-profile Turkish officials and international analysts speak of increased Turkish economic and military self-sufficiency and a relative decline of U.S. influence in the region as other actors become more consequential.[13]

Although Turkey is an increasingly important regional and even global player in the use of its political, economic, and cultural influence, many of its national security priorities remain concentrated on (1) protecting its borders and population, especially from the transnational threat posed by Kurdish militants; and (2) deterring would-be aggressors in its neighborhood without provoking them. Its defense cooperation with the United States, therefore, presents a dilemma. Avoiding provocations of those of Turkey's neighbors whom the United States perceives as adversaries or potential adversaries might be difficult for Turkey to the extent that the neighbors view Turkey as enabling U.S. actions in the region.

Cooperation During the Obama Administration

In General

Developments during the Obama Administration on matters both bilateral and under the NATO umbrella have led to new questions about the extent to which Turkish and U.S. national security goals and defense priorities overlap. In April 2009, President Obama, speaking of a "model partnership," visited Turkey during his first presidential trip abroad and addressed the Turkish Grand National Assembly (Parliament) in Ankara, saying that "Turkey is a critical ally.... And Turkey and the United States must stand together—and work together—to overcome the challenges of our time."

One month later, Ahmet Davutoglu, a foreign policy academic-turned-advisor to Prime Minister Recep Tayyip Erdogan from Turkey's ruling Justice and Development Party (AKP), became Turkey's foreign minister, giving Davutoglu greater visibility with regard to the more independent and assertive Turkish foreign policy course he had helped to establish. This course envisions Turkey being "in the centre of its own sphere of influence" through "strategic depth" (based largely on regional soft power ostensibly based on geopolitical, cultural, historical, and economic influence) and having "zero problems" with the countries in its vicinity.[14]

Subsequent Turkish and U.S. actions and statements on Armenia, Iran, and Israeli-Palestinian issues revealed tensions between the Obama Administration and AKP government visions for overcoming regional challenges. These tensions spilled over into bilateral defense relations.[15] In March 2010, the House Committee on Foreign Affairs reported H.Res. 252 for consideration by the full House (by a vote of 23-22). H.Res. 252 characterized actions of the Ottoman Empire (Turkey's predecessor state) against Armenians from 1915 to 1917 as genocide. Similar resolutions had been reported multiple times by the same committee for full House consideration since 2000, and by various House and Senate committees from 1984 to 1990. Neither H.Res. 252

nor any of the other resolutions passed. Nevertheless, in response to the March 2010 committee action, Turkey recalled its ambassador from the United States for one month, and at least one prominent AKP lawmaker reportedly warned that "the relationship would be downgraded on every level" in the event of House passage of the resolution (which as stated above, did not occur). This warning was commonly perceived as including a threat to at least partially or temporarily curtail U.S. access to Turkish bases and territory that it uses to transport non-lethal cargo to military missions in Iraq and Afghanistan.[16] Turkey also had briefly recalled its ambassador from the United States after a nearly identical resolution was reported by the same committee in October 2007.

Then, in May and June 2010, two developments raised significant concerns regarding TurkeyU.S. defense relations:

1) Turkey's Iranian nuclear diplomacy with Brazil—the Tehran Declaration on possible nuclear fuel swaps, followed by the Turkey-Brazil "no" vote on U.N. Security Council enhanced sanctions on Iran in Resolution 1929.
2) The *Mavi Marmara* Gaza flotilla incident and its aftermath, which publicly exacerbated the Turkey-Israel tensions that had been worsening since Israel's military operations in Hamas-controlled Gaza in December 2008.[17]

Some Members of Congress and Administration officials, viewing Turkey's rhetoric and actions as (1) undermining a top U.S. priority in the Iranian nuclear issue and (2) being at odds with the U.S. characterization of Israel as an ally and Iran as a threat, openly questioned Turkey's orientation on global security issues. Philip Gordon, U.S. Assistant Secretary of State for European and Eurasian Affairs, said in June 2010,

> We think Turkey remains committed to NATO, Europe and the United States, but that needs to be demonstrated. There are people asking questions about it in a way that is new, and that in itself is a bad thing that makes it harder for the United States to support some of the things that Turkey would like to see us support.[18]

Officials' and analysts' questions about Turkey's foreign policy direction intensified following reports that the 2010 version of the Turkish National Security Policy Document (MGSB, also known as the "Red Book") downgraded or did not explicitly list possible threats from Iran, Syria, Greece, and

Armenia that were listed in previous versions, and at the same time reportedly defined Israel's actions in the region as a threat—claiming that these actions induce conditions of instability.[19]

Turkey's alignment has major global implications and is driven by a variety of factors, including the AKP government's activist foreign policy.[20] The United States has limited influence over these factors. One of the main U.S. levers could be its ability to boost Turkey's short-term military capabilities (see "Arms Sales and Industrial Cooperation" below). However, the usefulness of such a lever could be fleeting, and its longer-term merits for regional security would be debatable. In the immediate aftermath of the Gaza flotilla incident and the U.N. Security Council Iran sanctions vote, the resulting prospect of greater congressional scrutiny of Turkey's objectives and actions reportedly led President Obama to warn Turkish Prime Minister Erdogan of the difficulty of gaining congressional approval for potential foreign military sales (FMS) of weapons systems—including drone aircraft—Turkey has reportedly sought for use against the Kurdistan Workers' Party (PKK, a U.S.-designated Foreign Terrorist Organization).[21] In this political climate, speculation arose about the possibility of increased support in Congress and the Administration for H.Res. 252 or another resolution or presidential statement regarding Armenian genocide claims.[22]

U.S. concerns about Turkey's position on Iran were somewhat allayed at the November 2010 NATO summit in Lisbon, Portugal, when Turkey joined its allies in approving a new strategic concept that specified the defense of territory and populations from ballistic missiles as a NATO mission. Separately, however, no decision has been announced on whether Turkey will agree to host a U.S. forward-deployed radar as a key element in the first phase of the Obama Administration's European Phased Adaptive Approach (EPAA) to missile defense. The Administration's timeline for the EPAA calls for such a radar to be deployed in southeastern Europe by the end of 2011,[23] and the *Wall Street Journal* reported in October 2010 that Turkey "is the location of choice ... according to military analysts and diplomats."[24] At the Lisbon summit, Turkey joined in the consensus of all NATO allies welcoming the EPAA as a "valuable national contribution to the NATO missile defense architecture," along with "other possible voluntary contributions by allies."[25] Thus, the question of the radar's deployment is important for both U.S. and NATO missile defense plans. U.S. and other international perceptions of Turkish cooperation on Iran may also improve following Turkey's March 2011 interdiction of two Iranian cargo planes en route to Syria over its airspace, from one of which Turkish officials reportedly confiscated a weapons cache pursuant to the U.N. Security Council embargo on Iranian arms exports and its enforcement mechanisms promulgated in Resolutions 1747 and 1929.[26]

On Libya and NATO's Role

As political unrest has spread throughout the Middle East in early 2011, President Obama has consulted frequently with Turkish Prime Minister Erdogan on political change in Egypt and other events occurring in the region. Following the passage of U.N. Security Council Resolution 1973 on March 17, 2011, which provided an international mandate to protect Libyan civilians,[27] the United States, France, and the United Kingdom began armed intervention in Libya against forces loyal to Muammar al Qadhafi's regime, initially repelling a planned assault on the Qadhafiopposition stronghold of Benghazi.

Turkey's position regarding NATO's role in the intervention has become increasingly important given both its geographical closeness to Libya and its status as a Muslim-majority country with significant cultural and historical ties to Libya. Before passage of Resolution 1973, Erdogan publicly opposed the idea of NATO involvement in Libya. Even though he criticized Qadhafi's violent suppression of protests and the incipient uprising and advocated a transfer of power in accord with Libyan citizens' wishes, Erdogan sought to facilitate a peaceful transfer of power through consultation with Qadhafi and Libyan opposition forces. After the passage of Resolution 1973 and the initial U.S.-led intervention, however, Turkey decided to help implement the resolution as part of a NATO-led coalition, after playing a major role in deliberations with the United States and other key allies.

Rather than a ratification of its allies' prior actions outside of NATO, Turkish leaders' support for and active participation in NATO's involvement in Libya appears to be a calculated decision both (1) to keep the scope of Western military involvement limited by actively steering NATO's political and operational decision-making processes, based on Turkey's interpretation of U.N. Security Council Resolution 1973; and (2) to avoid exclusion from a prominent role in brokering a resolution to the crisis.[28] On March 23, Turkish President Abdullah Gul said the following about pre-NATO actions in Libya:

> [T]he aim (of coalition forces) is not the liberation of the Libyan people. There are hidden agendas and differing interests. I worry that the things that happened in Iraq may be repeated in Libya....
>
> Everything should have been planned beforehand. What will be done against Gaddafi? How will the Libyan opposition be involved? Will there

> be a ground operation? All these should have been decided in NATO. But some decided to act with opportunist intentions and start a fire instead.[29]

Turkish Prime Minister Erdogan and Foreign Minister Davutoglu have indicated that Turkish forces will not undertake a combat role and that, as military operations continue, Turkey wants continual political consultation both among members of the NATO-led coalition and among the coalition, United Nations, Arab League, and African Union. Turkish officials have publicly stated their desire for a cease-fire as soon as possible that will allow the Libyan people to determine their own political future. Other NATO member states have also expressed concerns and set conditions for their involvement.

The parameters Turkey and other NATO allies have set for maintaining the NATO-led coalition, based on their respective interpretations of the international legitimacy of NATO's intervention under Resolution 1973, could compromise the room for strategic maneuver of the United States and certain other allies if events lead them to believe that more offensive action against Qadhafi's forces or the regime itself is advisable in order to avoid a protracted civil war. In that case, the United States and like-minded coalition members could ultimately be compelled to choose between their desired objectives and the possible alienation or even defection of Turkey and other actors from the coalition.[30]

The Turkish Parliament voted on March 24—less than three months before national elections planned for June—to permit the use of Turkish ground, air, and naval forces in Libya for up to a year pursuant to the terms of U.N. Security Council Resolution 1973 and its precursor, Resolution 1970. Erdogan announced on March 27 that Turkey would take direct responsibility for three humanitarian-assistance-related tasks within the NATO-led coalition: "the takeover of Benghazi airport for the delivery of humanitarian aid, the task about control of the air corridor and the involvement of Turkish naval forces in the corridor between Benghazi and Crete."[31]

Reportedly, Turkey is contributing at least six ships to NATO's naval fleet to enforce the Libya arms embargo—four frigates, a submarine, and an auxiliary warship. In addition, the aerial mission is being commanded from Turkey at NATO's Allied Air Component Command in Izmir (see Figure 1), and Turkey has contributed at least 10 aircraft to support the arms embargo and humanitarian assistance efforts.[32]

Defense News has speculated that designating the Izmir command center for use in Operation Unified Protector could influence whether it survives a reform process debated by many NATO member states that is aimed at streamlining the alliance's command structure:

> Turkey and NATO, only a few weeks ago, disputed a NATO plan to close down its air command center in Izmir, despite strong Turkish objections.
>
> Turkish Defense Minister Vecdi Gonul in early March said that "Turkey would struggle hard against such a plan."
>
> Some analysts think assigning Izmir as a sub-command structure for the Libyan mission may strengthen the Turkish case. A final decision on the future of the Izmir [command center] will be made at a NATO summit in June.[33]

It is not known whether the fate of NATO's Izmir command center was explicitly discussed or negotiated during the deliberations that led to Turkey's approval of and participation in Operation Unified Protector, but according to the Atlantic Council's "NATO Source" blog, efforts by NATO Secretary General Anders Fogh Rasmussen to convince Turkey to agree to the command center's closure during an early April trip to Ankara were unsuccessful.[34]

Military's Changing Role in Turkish Society

Since the formative days of the Turkish republic under Mustafa Kemal Ataturk in the 1920s and 1930s, the Turkish military has played a predominant role not only in Turkey's external defense,[35] but also in forging unity (often, in the early republican years, by helping implement Ataturk's reforms throughout the country) and keeping internal order. As the guarantor of stability, Turkey's military intervened in 1960, 1971, and 1980 to replace governments that it deemed had lost control of the country or had steered it away from the foundational secular republican principles established by Ataturk in the 1920s.[36]

The military's preeminence within the Turkish government and society at large gave it primacy over its civilian counterparts in bilateral and NATO defense cooperation matters with the United States. As longtime Turkey analyst Gareth Jenkins has explained,

> In theory, the [Turkish military hierarchy, known as the Turkish General Staff or TGS] is subordinate to the Prime Ministry. In practice, it is autonomous.

The Ministry of National Defense (MND) has no authority over the TGS, and its responsibilities are confined to conscription, defence procurement and relations with other ministries.

In Turkish protocol the chief of staff ranks ahead of the Minister of National Defence and second only to the prime minister.[37]

In the years since the 1980 military coup reestablished Turkish internal stability, the following interrelated factors have contributed to the relative weakening of the military's position within Turkish government and society:

- The subsequent liberalization of the Turkish economy contributed to the economic and political empowerment of a middle class drawn from traditional Turkish communities and largely sympathetic to Islamic values.
  A consequent increase in populist sentiment has posed political challenges to the military and to other so-called guardians of Turkey's secular elite (including academia and the judiciary).
- The Islamic-leaning Justice and Development Party (AKP) won a parliamentary majority in 2002 and subsequently enacted reforms strengthening civilian democratic institutions, sometimes at the military's expense, in line with EU accession requirements.[38]
  In 2007 national elections, the AKP garnered 12% more of the vote than it received in 2002.[39]
- The failed attempts or purported attempts by elements within the military, the judiciary, the opposition Republican People's Party (CHP), and others within the so-called Turkish secular elite to thwart the AKP on key issues. Events include

  - the 2007 election by Parliament of AKP member and former Prime Minister and Foreign Minister Abdullah Gul as Turkey's President;
  - the alleged Ergenekon/Sledgehammer plots to undermine or overthrow the government;
  - the 2008 Constitutional Court case attempting to ban and dissolve the AKP; and
  - the September 2010 passage of amendments to the 1982 military-backed constitution in a nationwide referendum, increasing military and judicial accountability to civilian and democratic institutions.[40]

The Turkish Armed Forces (TSK) are commanded by the Chief of the Turkish General Staff (TGS), who, since August 2010, has been General Isik Kosaner[a] (pronounced koh-SHAW-ner). The Chief of TGS customarily serves a two-year term.

517,100 Est. total manpower
402,000 Turkish Land Forces (Army)
60,100 Turkish Navy
55,000 Turkish Air Forces

20 Age young men are required to enlist in military service *(for a 15-month term, subject to some exceptions)*

The Gendarmerie and Coast Guard come under Interior Ministry control in peacetime, but TGS command in wartime.

$15.5 billion 2011 Defense Budget *up approximately 8% from 2010*
1.9% of gross domestic product (GDP)
7.4% of total government budget
$4.5 billion procurement spending
$505 million research and development spending, 2009 *(up 46% from 2007)*

$2.3 billion 2009 Annual Defense Industry Revenue *(more than double the 2002 figure)*
$832 million 2009 Annual Defense and Civil Aviation Exports *(more than six times the 2001 figure)*

Equipment
- The TSK has traditionally equipped itself with U.S. aircraft; German submarines; and other ships, armored vehicles, missiles, helicopters, and light arms from various indigenous and foreign sources.
- Israel had been a key supplier of drone aircraft and aircraft upgrade systems before the recent deterioration of Turkey-Israel ties.
- Turkey's procurement objectives called for 50% indigenous defense production by the end of 2010, and Foreign Trade Minister Zefer Caglayan claimed in August 2010 that indigenous production reached 46% in 2009.

Modernization and reform plans
- Greater readiness in confronting both conventional and asymmetric (weapons of mass destruction, terrorism, sabotage, and organized crime) threats
- Rapid deployability and sustainability in high- and low-intensity conflicts
- Greater "jointness" with international partners
- 20%-30% reduction in the army's size

Key government bodies with purview over defense matters include
- **National Security Council (MGK)** Chaired by the President. Includes the Prime Minister, Chief of TGS, Minister of National Defense, Foreign Minister, Interior Minister, Justice Minister, Deputy Prime Ministers, and the commanders of the Land Forces, Navy, Air Forces, and Gendarmerie.
- **Supreme Military Council (YAS)** Chaired by the Prime Minister. Includes the Chief of TGS, Minister of National Defense, the three TSK service commanders, and other commanders of four-star rank. Meets every August to discuss promotions and the general administration and regulation of the military. During the 2010 meetings, civilian leaders blocked or delayed the promotion of several officers suspected of past involvement in plots against the government. Reports also say that the YAS's traditional practice of expelling or disciplining officers with ideological (particularly Islamist) tendencies has become increasingly rare.
- **Defense Industry Executive Committee (SSIK)** Approves all military procurement decisions, and includes the Prime Minister, Chief of TGS, Minister of National Defense, and the head of the separate procurement agency known as the Undersecretariat for Defense Industries (SSM).[b] Since 2004, the SSM has been headed by the U.S.-educated Murad Bayar, who has spearheaded the movement to promote greater indigenous defense production.[c] However, Bayar and the SSM are advocating for a memorandum of understanding or "vision document" to guide future U.S.-Turkey defense industrial cooperation. A promotional office affiliated with the SSM opened near Washington, DC in 2010; according to Turkish daily Today's Zaman, similar offices are planned to open soon in Europe (Belgium), the Persian Gulf (Qatar), and the Caucasus and Central Asia (either Azerbaijan or Turkmenistan).

The traditionally autonomous TSK is gradually coming under greater civilian control.

Sources: TSK website at http://www.tsk.tr/eng/index.htm; *Jane's Sentinel Security Assessment - Eastern Mediterranean*, December 16, 2010; October 2010 American-Turkish Council annual conference at http://www.the-atc.org/events /c10 /presentations/Wednesday-Bfast-Lutfi-Varoglu.pdf; *Today's Zaman*; *Hurriyet Daily News & Economic Review*; *Eurasia Daily Monitor*.

[a] For a biography of General Kosaner, see NATO's website at http://www.nato.int /cps/en/SID-40C23228- 9940A075/natolive/who_is_who_65978.htm.

[b] The SSM was established in 1985 pursuant to Turkish Law No. 3238. According to its website, it has a separate legal entity, and has broad authority (1) to carry out the SSIK's decisions and (2) to organize and coordinate research and development, planning, production, and export and offset strategy for the Turkish defense industry. The SSM also has complete control over the Defense Industry Support Fund, which is separate from the annual defense budget. The Fund receives direct "allotments from corporate taxes, fees and levies imposed on alcoholic and tobacco products, and all forms of lottery, betting and games of chance etc." See http://www.ssm.gov.tr/home /institutional/Sayfalar/law3238.aspx.

[c] June 2009 *Defense News* profile of Bayar is available at chttp://www.defensenews. com /story.php?i=4160708.

Figure 2.Turkey's Military and Defense Establishment – Facts and Figures.

Preparations for the first external audit of Turkish defense spending in 2011, reported by *Jane's Sentinel Security Assessment*, further demonstrate the gradual subjection of military autonomy to civilian oversight.[41] Some Turkish analysts assert that curbs on the military's control over spending, involvement in the defense industry, and power as an economic actor through its large pension fund (known by its Turkish acronym OYAK) would need to go even further to make the military sufficiently democratically accountable.[42]

MAJOR AREAS OF DEFENSE COOPERATION

U.S.-Turkey defense cooperation continues apace with respect to promoting stability and countering terrorism in Iraq and Afghanistan. A U.S. defense presence in Turkey also continues— both through NATO and under the terms of a 1980 Defense and Economic Cooperation Agreement (DECA)[43]—as do joint defense consultations, training, and military exercises. Finally, Turkey continues to seek advanced military equipment from the U.S. government and private sector (i.e., fighter aircraft, drone aircraft, helicopters, and missile defense systems), and its defense industry participates in joint ventures with the United States (e.g., on the F-35 Joint Strike Fighter). However, Turkey's growing defense industry and its increased willingness to engage in arms import-export transactions or joint military exercises with non-NATO countries, such as China, Russia, Syria, Pakistan, and South Korea, indicate Turkey's interest in diversifying its defense relationships and de-creasing its dependence on the United States, consistent with the more independent foreign policy the AKP government is pursuing. These and additional areas of cooperation are discussed below.

NATO

Turkey's Future Role

With the second-largest military in NATO (the United States has the largest), its geographic location at the southeastern flank of the alliance, and its status as a Muslim-majority country, Turkey plays a strategically important role in NATO. Having been in the alliance since 1952, the structure, per-sonnel, and interoperability of its armed forces have been influenced over generations by its North American and European NATO partners. Turkey generally participates in NATO's expeditionary missions, including those in

Bosnia-Herzegovina, Kosovo, Afghanistan, and now Libya. As Turkey's defense spending remains robust while several European NATO member states reduce theirs, its relative weight within the alliance could grow over time. However, Turkey's current ability to devote its military manpower to NATO missions is somewhat compromised by ongoing commitments near its southeast border with Iraq, in the Aegean Sea region, and in northern Cyprus to protect the de facto republic for ethnic Turks there.

From Turkey's standpoint, its growing regional influence justifies greater Turkish involvement in setting and steering NATO's objectives and rules in a changing international environment.[44]

Turkey has shown assertiveness on many issues within the alliance in recent years, and this trend continued—if not intensified—during the March 2011 NATO deliberations over intervention in Libya.

In some aspects, Turkey perceives itself and is perceived as an anomaly within NATO, even if it remains firmly anchored in the alliance.[45] First, decades-long Turkish-Greek disputes over Cyprus (described above) and the Aegean Sea[46] have limited NATO's interoperability in the eastern Mediterranean and with the European Union (EU; of which Cyprus became a member in 2004). Additionally, the perception of Turkey as an outsider within NATO has been reinforced by the reluctance of at least some European countries to consider enforcing Turkey's Article 5 defense guarantees[47] during the run-up to the U.S.-led wars in Iraq in 1991 and 2003, and—perhaps even more fundamentally—to support Turkey's accession into the EU. In June 2010, U.S. Secretary of Defense Robert Gates said,

> I personally think that if there is anything to the notion that Turkey is, if you will, moving eastward, it is, in my view, in no small part because it was pushed, and pushed by some in Europe refusing to give Turkey the kind of organic link to the West that Turkey sought.
>
> I think we have to think long and hard about why these developments in Turkey [occurred] and what we might be able to do to counter them.[48]

When differences over NATO priorities arise between Turkey and its allies, they generally exacerbate the tensions within the alliance that are linked with long-running perceptions about Turkey. With regard to Libya, Turkish Foreign Minister Ahmet Davutoglu voiced concern about the precedent that individual NATO member states acting without greater international consultation might set for future cases, even though the decision to intervene in Libya came after the passage of U.N. Security Council Resolution 1973 and Arab League approval-in-principle of a no-fly zone:

> If a coalition will be formed, it must be coordinated by the UN. The UN Secretary General must convene a meeting. This is why the way the Paris meeting [between the United States, United Kingdom, and France] was held was contrary to international norms and customary practices. A group of countries cannot simply interpret a UN resolution in their own way and organize a military intervention in any country. If states that have formed a coalition among themselves are allowed to intervene against countries they target, that may lead to troubling situations in, say, the Middle East.[49]

Differences between Turkey and other NATO allies on intervention in Libya prompted one Western diplomat to say, "With its constant favoritism of fellow Muslim regimes in the Middle East, Turkey looks like a non-member NATO member—officially in but practically outside the alliance."[50] Such observations could reflect the difficulty some NATO countries might have in discerning to what extent Turkish policies are driven by possible cultural or ideological affinities, and to what extent they are driven by Turkey's desire to minimize the problems it faces given its geographical closeness—unique within NATO—to many ongoing areas of instability and conflict. Additionally, given the multiplicity of long-running disagreements within NATO that recur along regional, cultural, and other lines, it is possible that characterizations of Turkey as a NATO outlier or outsider might be overstated.

Missile Defense

As discussed above, Turkey and its NATO allies approved ballistic missile defense (BMD) for territories and populations as an alliance-wide mission at the November 2010 Lisbon summit. In exchange for its approval, Turkey reportedly insisted on the following two conditions:

1) No country (such as Iran or Syria) be named as a threat or a target for the ballistic missile defense system.
2) Turkey's territory would be entirely protected by the system.[51]

Discussions are apparently continuing between the United States and Turkey on the possibility of Turkey hosting a transportable U.S. radar,[52] as part of the European Phased Adaptive Approach (EPAA) that is planned to be part of a NATO BMD system and has been welcomed by NATO member states. Ian Lesser of the German Marshall Fund of the United States wrote, shortly after the Lisbon summit, that EPAA Standard Missile-3 interceptors (also known as the "Aegis" system) supported by a radar based in Turkey "would be based at sea, and eventually in Romania and Poland. All of this will be accompanied by new national air defense investments, including systems Turkey already plans to acquire."[53] For additional information on Turkey's possible acquisition of missile defense systems, see "Missile Defense Systems" below.

Turkey might decide that hosting a U.S. radar as part of an EPAA BMD system under the NATO umbrella would not be unduly provocative to countries such as Iran because the system is not designed for first-strike use and because Turkey has been considering missile defense options on its own and with the United States since at least 2001.[54] Hosting the radar could be justified domestically as cost effective and NATO-interoperable, particularly if Turkey can argue to its citizens that doing so will deliver tangible security benefits to them. On the other hand, Turkey, though it opposes the idea of Iranian nuclear weapons, has thus far publicly presumed that Iran's nuclear program is intended for purely peaceful, civilian means. If it believes that agreeing to host a U.S. radar as part of a NATO BMD system would lead Iran to perceive that Turkey's presumption about its nuclear program has changed, Turkey may be reluctant to risk a possible provocation. Turkey's active diplomatic role on the Iranian nuclear issue could have implications for the various actors' threat perceptions as well. It is unclear what connection Turkey sees between the arsenal of Turkey-based U.S. tactical nuclear weapons established under the NATO umbrella, if reports about the arsenal's existence are accurate (see "Bases and Transport Corridors" below),[55] and the political, strategic, or operational value of possible BMD elements in Turkey.[56] In the event Turkey does not host the proposed radar, the *Washington Post* has reported that Bulgaria might be asked to host it.[57]

Assuming Turkey accepts deployment of the radar on its territory in principle, it may still need to negotiate and implement the details of the arrangement with the United States. Assuming also that the EPAA is eventually implemented as part of a NATO BMD system, contingency planning for defense against missile attacks under various scenarios may generate differences of opinion between Turkey, the United States, and other allies about the proper NATO response.[58]

Afghanistan

Turkey has twice commanded the International Security Assistance Force (ISAF) in Afghanistan and has had troops participating in ISAF since shortly after its inception in December 2001. Turkey's approximately 2,000 troops concentrate on training Afghan military and security forces and providing security in Kabul, where Turkey commands ISAF's Regional Command-Capital, as well as in Wardak (just west of Kabul) and Jawzjan (in northern Afghanistan) provinces. According to the Turkish government,

- Turkey has made available its Konya Air Base and other airports for the deployment of [Airborne Warning & Control System (AWACS)] aircraft and allies' cargo aircraft in support of ISAF operations;
- Turkey has deployed five Operational Mentoring and Liaison Teams (OMLT) and has also conducted in-place training of 8,000 Afghan National Army (ANA) members and training in Turkey for an additional 1,000 ANA members; and
- Turkey established two civilian-led Provincial Reconstruction Teams (PRTs) in Wardak and Jawzjan, and opened a branch of the Turkish International Cooperation Agency in Kabul, from which it runs a number of humanitarian assistance and economic development projects.[59]

As with several other NATO and non-NATO contributors to ISAF, Turkey's troops are not involved in combat. Turkey's history of good relations with both Afghanistan and Pakistan and its status as the Muslim-majority country with the greatest level of involvement in ISAF is thought by some analysts to help legitimize ISAF's presence. It is unclear how Turkey's participation in the expeditionary mission to Afghanistan might translate into possible benefits for the United States and its other NATO allies in leveraging Turkey's possible cultural or ideological affinities for other potential defense cooperation contexts involving Muslim-majority countries located closer to Turkey's borders.[60]

Iraq

Pursuing Stability and Countering Iranian Influence

U.S.-Turkey defense cooperation in Iraq takes place within a larger context of questions about Iraq's future stability, political makeup, and regional profile. The United States plans to withdraw its troops by the end of 2011 and transition its military mission to Iraq under DOD auspices to a training and security assistance mission under State Department auspices. As it has begun to do so, Turkey has become more engaged politically and economically throughout the country, not only its traditional sphere of interest in the north.[61] It has contributed a modest contingent of personnel to the NATO Training Mission-Iraq since 2005 and has sponsored specialized training for hundreds of Iraqi security personnel at its NATO Partnership for Peace Training Center in Ankara.[62] Many analysts wonder whether the U.S. draw-down will compel Turkey to adopt a more vigorous approach backed by military strength with regard to countering Iranian influence and promoting stability.

Neutralizing the PKK?

Background

As mentioned above, Turkey—whose population is approximately 20% Kurdish—has struggled for nearly three decades with the PKK, a Kurdish separatist militant group and U.S.-designated Foreign Terrorist Organization that has implemented several attacks within Turkey since the mid-1980s. PKK attacks mushroomed and Kurdish secessionist sentiment within Turkey caused concerns in the 1990s following the establishment of an autonomous Kurdish zone in northern Iraq at the end of the 1991 Gulf War. Reported U.S. collaboration with Turkey helped it capture PKK leader Abdullah Ocalan in 1999, and the PKK declared a cease-fire shortly afterwards. After the 2003 Iraq war further strengthened Kurdish autonomy in Iraq, however, the PKK resumed operations against Turkish targets, using safe havens in northern Iraq. PKK leadership has spoken of changing the organization's ultimate goal to "autonomy" rather than outright secession. Turkish perceptions of U.S. culpability for the PKK threat were reinforced by U.S. and Iraqi efforts preventing Turkey from stationing troops in northern Iraq (after the United States originally suggested the stationing of Turkish troops, then reversed course following Iraqi protestations) during and after the 2003 war to monitor developments, control refugee flows, and protect Turkoman minorities (especially in Mosul and Kirkuk).

According to the State Department's Country Reports on Terrorism for 2009, the PKK maintains a regular fighting force of approximately 4,000-5,000 militants. Of those, 3,000-3,500, including the organization's military leadership, are thought to be concentrated in the Qandil mountains of northern Iraq. The PKK has a branch dedicated to attacks on military targets in southeastern Turkey, and a branch dedicated to attacks (primarily bombings) in urban, primarily tourist areas in western Turkey.[63] Estimates of casualties from Turkey-PKK violence since 1984 range from 32,000 to 45,000 (including armed combatants and civilians on both sides),[64] the majority of whom were killed during the 1990s. Hundreds of thousands of Kurdish villagers in southeastern Turkey have been displaced as a result of the violence, and Kurdish human rights grievances persist.[65]

Turkey once viewed the Kurdistan Regional Government (KRG) in northern Iraq as a primary PKK enabler. Increasingly, however, KRG officials welcome the stability they view Turkish investment as bringing to the region and have become tolerant of Turkish efforts to counter the PKK, though they claim that they are militarily incapable and politically constrained from actively halting or disrupting PKK operations themselves. Syria, which used to provide safe haven to the PKK, stopped doing so in 1999 after its expulsion of Abdullah Ocalan. Iran occasionally cooperates with Turkey against the PKK because of problems with its own Kurdish minority.[66]

U.S. Support of Turkish Efforts

After two major PKK cross-border ambushes in southeastern Turkey killed 25, injured 20, and captured 8 Turkish soldiers in October 2007, Turkey amassed approximately 100,000 troops on its border with Iraq.[67] To persuade the Turks not to undertake a full-scale cross-border invasion, which could have imperiled U.S. supply lines to Iraq from Turkey and overall regional stability, the Bush Administration reportedly agreed to close counterterrorism cooperation involving real-time intelligence sharing on the location and movement of PKK operatives. As reported by the *Washington Post* in December 2007,

> U.S. military personnel have set up a center for sharing intelligence in Ankara, the Turkish capital, providing imagery and other immediate information gathered from U.S. aircraft and unmanned drones flying over the separatists' mountain redoubts, the officials said. A senior administration official said the goal of the U.S. program is to identify the movements and activities of the Kurdish Workers' Party (PKK), which is fighting to create an autonomous enclave in Turkey.
>
> The United States is "essentially handing them their targets," one U.S. military official said. The Turkish military then decides whether to act on the information and notifies the United States, the official said.[68]

Jane's Sentinel Security Assessment reported that, starting in December 2007, "The US assisted with the co-ordination of the air strikes by allowing the aircraft into Iraqi airspace. The air strikes were supported by ground-based artillery fired from within Turkey." Other than a brief incursion in February 2008 and other minor raids, regular Turkish ground forces have not crossed the border. Jane's said that Turkish officials told it that the air strikes are insufficient to stop the PKK's operations, but do help "in intimidating the PKK and discouraging infiltration into Turkey."[69] Thus, future Turkish ground operations remain a possibility, depending on factors such as

- Iraqi national government and KRG approval and support, and
- the effectiveness of non-military (i.e., political and socioeconomic) approaches to ameliorating tensions involving Turkey's Kurds.

The United States has encouraged Turkey-Iraq-KRG coordination on these matters. This coordination is likely to become a more significant factor as the United States draws down its own presence. U.S. officials, both civilian and military, also routinely emphasize the ultimate importance of non-military means, which the AKP government has tried to a limited extent in considering a variety of measures for Kurds, such as greater local governance, linguistic rights, and cultural rights.

The so-called "Kurdish opening" or "democratic initiative" stalled in 2009 in the face of criticism from opposition parties as well as the closure (or dissolution) of the predominantly Kurdish Democratic Society Party (DTP) by Turkey's Constitutional Court. The DTP's place in Turkish politics has since been taken by the Peace and Democracy Party (BDP).

Renewed PKK attacks in the spring and summer of 2010 killed approximately 100 Turkish security force and military personnel, drawing frequent cross-border retaliatory air and artillery strikes from U.S.-aided Turkish forces. Although it remains unclear, one of the PKK's offshoots may have been culpable in an October 2010 suicide bombing in Istanbul's main Taksim Square that injured 32 people.

Because this is the high-profile national security issue with which the Turkish military is most operationally involved, many analysts view the prestige of the Turkish military as increasingly bound up with ending PKK attacks.

The centrality of the issue, along with the Turkish perception of the United States as responsible for the problem and uniquely positioned to help counter it, makes it the focus of Turkey's most urgent defense cooperation requests.

The shrinking timeline for U.S. military operations in Iraq has possibly heightened this sense of urgency among Turks who believe that U.S.-Turkey counterterrorism cooperation may be affected by the reduced U.S. footprint and thus seek an effective alternative.

Incirlik Air Base

Incirlik (pronounced in-JUR-lick) air base is an enduring symbol of U.S.-Turkey defense cooperation. Constructed in the 1950s by the U.S. Army Corps of Engineers in southern Turkey outside the major city of Adana (now Turkey's fifth-largest city, with a population of 1.6 million), Incirlik's two runways eventually became a key hub for U.S. and NATO training and reconnaissance missions during the Cold War. The Turkish air force took possession of Incirlik at the outset of the 1975- 1978 U.S. arms embargo, but NATO operations continued. U.S. operations resumed after the embargo, with the base under overall Turkish control. Since the end of the Cold War, Incirlik has been used most notably by the U.S. Air Force and other NATO allies for operations in Iraq and Afghanistan. Although bases in the Persian Gulf and Central Asia have lightened Incirlik's U.S. traffic, supply and refueling operations continue, and, as discussed in the report, Incirlik is the reported location of the U.S. tactical nuclear weapons arsenal in Turkey under NATO auspices.

As the U.S. military presence in Turkey has decreased from its peak of some 25,000 personnel in the late 1960s, and has been completely vacated from several installations, many veterans and U.S. officials familiar with the legacy of U.S.-Turkey defense cooperation view Incirlik as the legacy's continuing bellwether.

Bases and Transport Corridors

Under the U.S.-Turkey Defense and Economic Cooperation Agreement, the United States maintains access to a few Turkish installations for its military use. It stations over 1,700 U.S. military personnel in Turkey, and employs approximately 5,500 total personnel, counting local workers. The largest U.S. presence is at Incirlik air base in southern Turkey near the city of Adana, with approximately 1,500 U.S. personnel (5,000 total, including Turkish contractors). According to *The Bulletin of the Atomic Scientists*, Incirlik also is the reported home of vaults holding approximately 60-70 U.S. tactical, aircraft-deliverable B61 nuclear gravity bombs under NATO auspices.[70] Since the end of the Cold War, Incirlik has been used to support U.S. and NATO operations in Iraq, Bosnia-Herzegovina, Kosovo, and Afghanistan. The Air Force (39th Air Base Wing) uses Incirlik to provide non-lethal cargo to U.S. military missions in Iraq and Afghanistan. According to information provided by ODCAnkara in October 2010, the United States sends 68% of air logistical support for Iraq and Afghanistan through Incirlik, with C-17 aircraft flying an average of 2,000 sorties per year and KC-135 refueling aircraft an average of 1,460. U.S. European Command estimates that its use of Incirlik and its overflight of Turkish airspace saves approximately $210 million per year in alternate route costs. However, Turkey maintains the right to cancel U.S. access to Incirlik with three days' notice.

The United States has relied heavily on the Habur Gate, the only available land border crossing into northern Iraq, for the transport of fuel, subsistence, and construction materials to support U.S. military operations, but future needs are less clear with those operations drawing down. According to ODC-Ankara, the Mediterranean port of Mersin in southern Turkey is becoming an increasingly important point for the military to transport containerized cargo along the Northern Distribution Network (NDN) route from Turkey to Georgia and through the Caucasus and Central Asia to Afghanistan. As the United States draws down in Iraq, it uses the Habur Gate to "retrograde" non-lethal cargo and further transport it to Afghanistan along the NDN. The other U.S. military transportation corridor from Iraq to Afghanistan uses Kuwait, the Persian Gulf, and Pakistan to bypass Iran.

The U.S. Office of Defense Cooperation (ODC-Ankara), with approximately 30 U.S. personnel (100 total), is located in Ankara. Ankara is also home to two NATO training centers: the Partnership for Peace Training Center[71] and the Center of Excellence-Defense Against Terrorism.[72] Approximately 170 U.S. personnel (290 total) are located in the western Turkish city of Izmir to support NATO's Allied Air Component Command, the designated command center for the aerial mission in Libya for Operation Unified Protector (see "On Libya and NATO's Role" above). A contingent of approximately 17 U.S. personnel mans two air postal squadrons and a tactical management office in Istanbul. One of six NATO Rapid Deployable Corps is headquartered near Istanbul; the others are located in France, Germany (two), Italy, and Spain.

For locations of the U.S. and NATO presence in Turkey, see Figure 1 above.

POSSIBLE U.S. POLICY APPROACHES

Congress and other U.S. policymakers may choose from a range of possible approaches to action on and oversight of U.S. defense cooperation with Turkey. In considering options, Members of Congress could engage in formal and informal oversight and information-gathering through committee hearings and consultations with key actors within the executive branch, the Turkish government and defense establishment, and non-governmental and international organizations, including the NATO Parliamentary Assembly. Four possible approaches are described below, in no particular order of priority.

Status Quo Approach: *Would not focus significantly on recent developments, but rather emphasize and express confidence that existing NATO and bilateral relationships—with their long legacies—can address mutual security challenges, even in an evolving regional and global context.*

Those favoring this approach might argue that recent changes within and outside of Turkey should not change the overall parameters of the alliance. These advocates might present a historical view arguing that U.S.-Turkey defense relations, even during the Cold War, have experienced ups and downs, but that each side ultimately concludes that it needs the other and therefore a permanent rupture is unlikely in the future.

This approach would not advocate conditioning U.S. cooperation with Turkey on specific actions or relations with third-party countries. It would not acknowledge either a need to revisit institutional structures or decision-making processes, or the possibility that Turkish foreign policy stances in opposition to the United States could lead to a more mature and productive bilateral relationship in the long run.

Critics of a status quo approach, however, could argue that recent challenges to the U.S.-Turkey alliance are fundamentally different than past ones, and that a static view of the bilateral and NATO alliances in light of regional and global changes risks ceding initiative to other actors and leaving the United States unprepared for the potential consequences. Omer Taspinar, longtime analyst of U.S.-Turkey relations at the Brookings Institution, wrote in early 2011 of the possible risks if U.S. officials and analysts pay insufficient attention to changes in the alliance's dynamics:

> As France did under Charles de Gaulle in the 1960s, Turkey may opt for its own ... "Realpolitik" with countries such as China, India, and Russia. It could even contemplate leaving, as France under de Gaulle did, the military structure of NATO, while maintaining its political membership in the organization.[73]

Accommodative Approach: Accord high priority to the U.S.-Turkey alliance and revise expectations for it by accommodating Turkey's expressions of its national interests—and U.S. perceptions of these interests—given recent developments within Turkey, the region, and globally.[74]

By maintaining that the alliance is based broadly on shared values and interests such as long-term regional stability, rather than on any particular issue, Congress might acknowledge its dedication to cooperation even in the event Turkey opposes U.S. policies in certain cases.[75] Responsiveness to Turkish requests for arms to counter the PKK, Turkish conditions on hosting missile defense system elements, and Turkish desires to have a greater role in multilateral institutional structures and decision-making processes that address regional order would be possible despite ongoing Turkish disputes with Israel and Armenia, and despite Turkish relations with actors such as Iran, China, Syria, and Hamas. Under this approach Congress could still voice criticism of Turkey on issues affecting U.S. interests, but might generally avoid characterizing any such issue as a litmus test for the alliance.

Those supporting this approach might argue that Turkey is more likely to serve U.S. and NATO interests as an "independent" and "credible" regional actor than as an actor perceived as following Western dictates. Some analysts have argued that strong U.S. relations with democratically elected Turkish leaders is the best (or least-worst) option for forwarding regional U.S. interests and countering Iranian influence in places such as Iraq, regardless of U.S.-Turkey divergences on some issues.[76] A counterargument is that this approach would establish a bad precedent by ceding judgment to Turkey to determine whether an action or policy that appears to run contrary to U.S. interests (such as on Iran or Israel) is justified, and that it also constitutes tacit U.S. acceptance and even de facto sponsorship of Turkey's efforts to diversify its military contacts and import-export relationships with other countries, including China. In the absence of specifically prescribed limits to toleration of Turkish divergence from U.S. stances on key issues, this approach could be seen as an imprudent overcorrection.

Linkage Approach: Link cooperation to some extent to Turkey's relations with certain third-party countries or non-state actors—including Iran, Israel, Hamas, Armenia, and China—or to Turkish actions on issues of U.S. national security interest.[77]

Clear parameters for cooperation will arguably allow Turkey to demonstrate the importance it attaches to cooperation with the United States, depending on how closely it aligns its actions with U.S. interests. Recent U.S. differences with Turkey on the Iranian nuclear issue and other issues may have been caused or exacerbated by mutual misperceptions.[78] However, avoiding miscommunication might be difficult in any event given multiple congressional views that potentially conflict with each other and with Administration views on what parameters to set and how to set them.

On the other hand, this approach might lead Turkey to adopt the view that third-party countries or priority issues are more important to the United States than its alliance with Turkey. Firm congressional redlines or ultimatums could risk the relationship's future, particularly if Turkey chooses to challenge them, while giving ground on them could endanger U.S. credibility.

Case-by-Case Approach: Use or combine any of the other three approaches on a case-by-case basis.

Approach(es) to U.S.-Turkey defense cooperation matters could hinge on a number of factors, including the following:

- U.S.-Turkish agreement on how to address regional security challenges;
- Turkey's relations with key third-party countries and non-state actors, including Iran, Israel, Hamas, Armenia, China, Cyprus, and Greece;
- Turkey's perceived importance to U.S. interests given regional and global developments and trends, as well as possible alternate locations for military basing and transport corridors;
- the level of U.S. trust in Turkish leaders (civilian and military) and in internal Turkish stability; and
- the likelihood of influencing Turkey to act in U.S. interests and of strengthening the overall bilateral and NATO relationships.

Using a case-by-case approach, however, risks that Turkey and outside observers will characterize congressional action and oversight as inconsistent and unpredictable. It may have the advantage, however, of being responsive to changing developments in a region of the world that is of critical importance to U.S. national security.

Specific Issues and Possible Options for Congress

Access to Turkish Bases and Transport Corridors

The prospect of temporary or permanent denial of U.S. military access to Turkish bases and transport corridors concerns Congress and other policymakers. A loss of U.S. access to Incirlik air base and the closure of the Habur Gate and Mersin port could cause delays and increase costs for the transport of cargo to Afghanistan through alternate routes (see "Bases and Transport Corridors" above). Short-term costs and delays may be of less concern than the longer-term question of how a potential lack of access to Incirlik, other bases, and Turkish transport corridors could affect options for future U.S./NATO military action in the region, particularly if regional and global developments prevent or limit the United States from using alternate sites in the Persian Gulf, the Caucasus, Central Asia, or South Asia to stage operations or establish supply lines. Members of Congress might inquire whether additional alternatives to Turkish bases or transport corridors—within other NATO countries or elsewhere—might exist or be developed for use in the surrounding region.

Reaction to Downturn in Turkey-Israel Relations

A drop-off in Turkish military cooperation with Israel has taken place in parallel with a general deterioration of Turkey-Israel relations since 2009. This downturn can be attributed to a number of factors, including the May 2010 *Mavi Marmara* flotilla incident (mentioned above) and Turkish-Israeli differences over Israel's invasion of Hamas-controlled Gaza in December 2008. It also parallels the military's declining role in Turkish society, and the greater empowerment of Prime Minister Erdogan and other AKP and national leaders who seem increasingly to believe that criticizing many of Israel's policies is both merited and domestically popular.

The souring of Turkey-Israel relations has the potential to affect U.S.-Turkey defense cooperation given that the United States maintains close alliances with both Turkey and Israel (which is not a member of NATO), and has counted on previously close Turkey-Israel military relations to cultivate U.S.-Turkey-Israel military cooperation. Although Israel did complete the delivery to Turkey of already-purchased Heron drone aircraft after the flotilla incident, Turkey has ceased its participation in joint exercises with Israel, and new arms sales and defense industrial cooperation are on hold indefinitely pending the resolution of post-flotilla grievances. So far, neither country has pursued a resolution to the other's satisfaction. The air exercise Anatolian Eagle and the naval exercise Reliant Mermaid, both of which had featured U.S.-Turkey-Israel cooperation in previous years, did not feature either the

United States or Israel in late 2010. Anatolian Eagle took place with different participants, and Reliant Mermaid was canceled.

It also is unclear to what extent divergent Turkish and Israeli positions on regional issues involving Iran, the Palestinians, and other actors could lead to a further breach between the two and, by reason of U.S.-Israeli closeness, to further strains on U.S.-Turkey defense relations. For example, Turkey has reportedly set as one condition for its willingness to host a U.S. radar sensors as part of a ballistic missile defense system that information from the radar not be shared with Israel (which hosts a separate U.S. missile defense radar system).

Following the May 2010 flotilla incident, the Senate passed S.Res. 548 by voice vote on June 24, 2010. The resolution condemned the attack by the "extremists aboard the Mavi Marmara," invoked Israel's right to self-defense, and encouraged "the Government of Turkey to recognize the importance of continued strong relations with Israel and the necessity of closely scrutinizing organizations with potential ties to terrorist groups."[79] A January 2011 *New York Times Magazine* article quotes Selim Yenel, a Turkish Foreign Ministry deputy undersecretary responsible for U.S. relations, as saying, "We're getting a lot of flak from the Hill. We used to get hit by the Greek lobby and the Armenian lobby, but we were protected by the Jewish lobby. Now the Jewish lobby is coming after us as well."[80]

In the near term, an improvement in relations between the AKP government and the Israeli government of Prime Minister Binyamin Netanyahu does not appear likely. It is debatable whether an active U.S. brokering role will improve or worsen prospects for Turkey-Israel rapprochement and for future U.S. defense relations with both countries. Developments on this issue could have implications for how much future influence the United States has on regional security.

Missile Defense Radar and NATO

Construction and deployment of the various elements of the U.S. European Phased Adaptive Approach (EPAA) to ballistic missile defense in Europe, including a possible radar in Turkey, is subject to congressional appropriations and oversight.[81] The Joint Explanatory Statement of the House and Senate Armed Services Committees (the practical equivalent of a conference report) on the FY2011 Ike Skelton National Defense Authorization Act (P.L. 111-383) enacted on January 7, 2011,[82] contains the following:

- A provision conditioning the use of funds for construction and deployment of land-based interceptors of the EPAA on prior approval by the host nation(s) of the required basing and deployment agreements. This condition, however, is subject to waiver by the Secretary of Defense for national security reasons. Furthermore, the provision states that it is not intended to impede or delay the successful implementation of the EPAA, nor is it intended to limit the production of missile defense interceptors for ground- and flight-testing, or production validation.
- A provision that limits funds for construction and deployment of the land-based portion of the EPAA until after Congress receives an independent assessment of the operational and cost effectiveness of the EPAA as required by the FY2010 National Defense Authorization Act (P.L. 111-84).

In addition to being responsible for the costs of land- and sea-based EPAA deployment, which NATO welcomed at its November 2010 Lisbon Summit as a U.S. contribution to its territorial BMD system while awaiting operational integration, the United States is to be equally responsible with the other 27 NATO member states—through the common NATO budget—for the general costs of the BMD system. NATO Secretary General Anders Fogh Rasmussen has estimated these costs to be €200 million (about $260 million) over 10 years.[83]

The Administration's initial timeline for the EPAA calls for the radar to be deployed by the end of 2011. Congress, NATO allies, and other international actors could determine that it is important to ensure that the Administration meets its stated objective. The extent to which this will translate into time pressure on Turkey to decide on hosting the radar and conclude the necessary basing and deployment agreements with the United States is unclear. In addition to Turkish leaders' concerns about the EPAA's practical capabilities in defending their territory and people, other reservations reportedly "center on being included in the decision process for the system and sharing in its technological expertise."[84]

Arms Sales and Industrial Cooperation

Turkey no longer receives annual Foreign Military Financing aid for purchasing U.S.-produced equipment. Yet, partly due to the historical legacy established by its past reliance on U.S. assistance, and partly due to continued U.S. preeminence in advanced military technology, Turkey still considers the United States to be a preferred supplier of aircraft, helicopters, electronic warfare systems, and advanced missile systems through foreign military sales (FMS) or from U.S. defense contractors through direct commercial sales (DCS). However, Turkey's desire to limit its dependence on any one nation or group of nations has led to procurement and industrial cooperation policies that have come into tension with U.S. practices regarding co-production and technology sharing. As a result, Turkey increasingly solicits competitive offers from multiple countries for its defense acquisitions. It seriously considers offers from non-U.S. suppliers that may not be as technologically advanced or reliable, but that Turkey perceives as being more flexible in negotiations and in sharing expertise, and therefore more helpful in contributing to Turkey's long-term goal of industrial self-reliance. Other countries that Turkey considers as possible sources of procurement and/or partners in co-development include NATO countries such as Germany and Italy, plus others such as South Korea, Russia, China, Pakistan, Indonesia, Singapore, and South Africa.

See Appendix B for more detailed information on Turkey's procurement and defense industry policies.

Congressional Notification Process

For both FMS and DCS, the Arms Export Control Act (AECA) generally requires the executive branch to provide 15 days' formal notice to Congress before proceeding with the sale (for FMS) or issuing an export license (for DCS) for deals involving the sale of defense equipment valued at or above $25 million to NATO allies such as Turkey.[85] The executive branch may provide informal notification and briefings to Congress before giving formal notice. Subject to presidential veto, Congress may block FMS or DCS under expedited procedures permitted by the AECA at any time before the formal notice period elapses, or through separate legislation at any time before delivery of the defense article(s) in question.

In determining the advisability of potential arms sales to Turkey, Congress could take into account the

- capabilities and postures of other actors in the surrounding region; and
- historical and prospective utility of arms sales in serving U.S. interests compared with other means of influence (i.e., diplomacy, trade, cultural/educational ties, economic and humanitarian assistance).

Table 2. Significant U.S.-Origin Arms Transfers or Expected Arms Transfers to Turkey (congressional notifications since 2006)

Amount/Description	FMS or DCS	Year			Primary Contractor(s)	Estimated Cost
		Cong. Notice	Contract	Delivery		
100 F-35A Joint Strike	DCS	2006		2014-2023	Lockheed	$11-$15
Fighter aircraft (possibly 16 more discussed following congressional notice)				(Expected if contract signed)	Martin	billion
30 F-16C Block 50	FMS	2006	2009	By 2013	Consortium	$1.8 billion
Fighter aircraft and associated equipment				(Expected)	(Lockheed Martin, Raytheon, and others)	
48 AGM-84H SLAM-ER Air-surface missiles	FMS	2006	2006	Complete	Boeing	$162 million
105 AIM-9X	FMS	2007			Raytheon	$71 million
SIDEWINDER Air-air missiles (SRAAM)						
51 Block II Tactical	FMS	2007	2008 (for		McDonnell	$159
HARPOON Anti-ship missiles			at least 4)		Douglas (Boeing)	million
100 MK-54 MAKO Torpedoes	FMS	2007	2009	By 2012 (Expected)	Raytheon	$105 million
30 AAQ-33 SNIPER and AN/AAQ-13 LANTIRN	FMS	2008	2009		Lockheed Martin	$200 million
Aircraft electro-optical systems (targeting and navigation pods)						
6 MK 41 Vertical Launch	FMS	2008	Signed	3 already	Lockheed	$227
Systems for Ship-air missiles				3 by 2012 (Expected)	Martin	million
107 AIM-120C-7 Air-air missiles (AMRAAM)	FMS	2008	Signed	By 2012 (Expected)	Raytheon	$157 million

Amount/Description	FMS or DCS		Year		Primary Contractor(s)	Estimated Cost
		Cong. Notice	Contract	Delivery		
400 RIM-162 Ship-air missiles (ESSM)	DCS	2009			Raytheon	$300 million
72 PATRIOT Advanced	FMS	2009			Raytheon and	$4 billion
Capability Missiles (PAC-					Lockheed	
3), 197 PATRIOT					Martin	
Guidance Enhanced						
Missiles, and associated equipment						
14 CH-47F CHINOOK	FMS	2009			Boeing	$1.2 billion
Helicopters						

Source: Defense Security Cooperation Agency, Stockholm International Peace Research Institute Arms Transfer Database, *Defense News*, Global Security.

Notes: All figures and dates are approximate; blank entries indicate that data is unknown or not applicable.

Turkish officials are likely to expect congressional attitudes that are similarly favorable—if not more so—toward potential U.S. arms sales to Turkey as they are toward potential sales to other NATO and non-NATO allies. This may be the case even though Turkish officials may simultaneously expect the United States to have exceptional tolerance for Turkish policies that diverge from U.S. stances on key issues because of Turkey's unique geo-political position and demographics among U.S. allies.

Drones to Counter the PKK in Northern Iraq?

Turkey reportedly has sought since 2008 to purchase drone aircraft (also known as unmanned aerial systems (UASs) or vehicles (UAVs)) from the United States to assist in its counterterrorism efforts against the PKK.[86] In 2010, Turkey reportedly deployed up to 10 medium-altitude, long-endurance (MALE) Heron drones acquired from Israel in this effort, after production and delivery delays owing to Turkey-Israel tensions and technical problems with integrating Turkish-produced electro-optical equipment. According to *Jane's Sentinel Security Assessment*, in December 2008, Turkey requested an FMS purchase of 10 U.S.-produced MALE drones for use against the PKK: four General Atomics MQ-1 Predators and six MQ-9 Reapers, some of which would have armed capability.[87]

President Obama reportedly told Turkish Prime Minister Erdogan in June 2010 that Turkey's diplomacy with respect to the Iranian nuclear issue would make congressional approval for U.S. sales of drone aircraft to Turkey more difficult to obtain. With U.S. military operations in Iraq set to transition to a State Department-led security assistance effort by the end of 2011, it is unclear to what extent reported U.S. drone surveillance of PKK "mountain redoubts" in northern Iraq, such as those described by the *Washington Post* in December 2007 (see "Neutralizing the PKK?" above), will continue.

Questions about how to maintain stability around the Turkey-Iraq border and in the overall region could lead to greater public debate over how directly involved the United States should be and the potential costs and benefits of providing Turkey with more advanced military capabilities and technologies. Concerns include possible precedents for future arms sales or industrial cooperation involving Turkey or other allies and possible PKK retaliatory targeting of U.S. personnel and equipment in the region.

In light of the sensitive proprietary technology involved and potential concerns about end use, negotiating the sale of U.S. drone aircraft to Turkey could be an extremely complicated process. Yet, given U.S. responsibility for the PKK threat in the eyes of many Turks, and the importance they attach to countering the threat, delays or collapses of the process—however justifiable—are likely to result in perceptions of insufficient U.S. cooperation. The persistence of these perceptions could lead to even greater Turkish reliance on non-U.S. defense suppliers.

Fighter Aircraft

Turkey's air force is critical to its overall defense posture. Fighter aircraft purchased from the United States have long formed the core of the fleet. Most of Turkey's 240 Lockheed Martin F-16s were co-produced in Turkey by a predecessor firm of Turkish Aerospace Industries (TAI). In addition, after nearly two years of negotiations, the United States and Turkey signed an FMS contract in 2009 for 30 F-16 Block 50s to be co-produced by TAI. Delivery is expected by 2013. *Jane's Sentinel Security Assessment* estimated the cost of the deal (including engines, avionics, and associated weapons systems) to be $1.78 billion, although the September 2006 congressional notification from the Defense Security Cooperation Agency (DSCA) indicated that the cost, if all options were exercised, could be as high as $2.9 billion. *Jane's* also stated that a planned $200 million sale of 30 AN/AAQ-33 Sniper targeting pods and 30 AN/AAQ-13 LANTIRN extended range navigation pods is probably associated with the F-16 deal.[88]

Turkey is one of eight countries—along with the United Kingdom, Canada, Netherlands, Italy, Denmark, Norway, and Australia—partnering with the United States on the F-35 Joint Strike Fighter (JSF) program.[89] Turkey plans to purchase up to 116 F-35s,[90] for delivery over an estimated 10-year period (2014-2023), that are jointly assembled and/or developed by firms from the various JSF partners. The cost will be at least $11 billion and could exceed $15 billion, given continued cost inflation on the program. A final purchasing decision could be made in 2011. Turkish companies have received contracts to do substantial work that *Jane's* estimates could result in revenue between $5 billion-$6 billion over 20 years,[91] including a TAI contract with Northrop Grumman to be a second-source production center for up to 400 center fuselages, and a joint venture between U.S. firm Pratt and Whitney and Turkey's Kale Group to manufacture parts for JSF F135 engines.

Turkish officials have complained in the media about the difficulty of modernizing Turkey's F-16 fleet—particularly without Israel as an available supplier due to political tensions (see "Reaction to Downturn in Turkey-Israel Relations" above)—and of taking part in the JSF program due to disagreements with the United States over technology sharing and costs. It is unclear, however, whether Turkish expressions of dissatisfaction are likely to affect its industrial cooperation with the United States in the near term given (1) Turkish operational needs, (2) the boost the JSF program is likely to give the Turkish defense industry, and (3) the lack of alternatives. In December 2010, Turkey announced long-term plans to produce its own fighter aircraft after 2020, either by itself or with other countries on terms it deems more favorable.[92] It has discussed possible cooperation with South Korea and Indonesia, but Turkish daily *Today's Zaman* reported in January 2011 that Turkey may seek to create a fighter production consortium with Gulf countries.[93]

Missile Defense Systems

According to *Today's Zaman*, Turkey is seeking to purchase batteries for a Turkish Long Range Air and Missile Defense System, estimated to cost $4 billion, through a bidding process open to foreign companies.[94] The Turkish Defense Industry Executive Committee[95] will supposedly entertain bids from foreign companies in early 2011. U.S. defense contractor Raytheon is expected to offer its Patriot PAC-3 system:

> In this system, a 73-kilogram cluster and explosive warhead hits and destroys the targeted missile. Turkey is attracted by the fact that this system can be integrated with the Airborne Warning and Control System (AWACS) aircraft. However, the US administration is not keen on the idea of technology transfer with Patriots, and this certainly makes it difficult for Turkey to make a decision.[96]

Probable offers from Russian and Chinese companies, as well as the European consortium Eurosam, are also mentioned.[97] Whether Turkey will consider the tender offers in coordination with its decision on hosting a U.S. missile defense radar under NATO auspices (see “Missile Defense” above) is unclear. Both the Raytheon and Eurosam offers are expected to tout their NATO interoperability.

Military and Security Assistance

The United States does provide some annual military and security assistance to Turkey. In FY2010, Turkey received $5 million in International Military Education Training (IMET) aid and nearly $3 million in Non-proliferation, Anti-terrorism, Demining and Related Programs (NADR) aid. The Obama Administration's FY2011 and FY2012 requests for funding these accounts for Turkey, along with the International Narcotics Control and Law

Enforcement (INCLE) account, contemplates aiding a wide range of Turkish law enforcement, customs, and security agencies as well as the military (see Table 1 above).

In addition, Turkey has prior-year U.S. Foreign Military Financing (FMF) funds in the amount of approximately $75 million available to it from an account under U.S. government control. When Turkey might spend these unobligated funds remains unclear. DOD informed the Congressional Research Service in March 2011 that the most recent Turkish spending plan for these funds include these approximate allocations:

- Communications, $33.3 million;
- General equipment sustainment, $19 million;
- Oliver Hazard Perry-class frigate upgrades, $15 million; and
- Other equipment and systems, $7.7 million.

Monitoring Turkey's Joint Military Activities

Involving the United States and NATO

Turkey's joint exercises, operations, and use of bases with the United States could be a subject of congressional oversight. As discussed above, the United States maintains a regular presence at Turkey's Incirlik air base. Through NATO's auspices, it also maintains a presence at the Allied Air Component Command in Izmir, which was designated as the aerial command center for Operation Unified Protector in Libya. In addition, the United States and NATO maintain bases throughout Europe and North America where Turkey's military occasionally detaches troops and officers for joint use, consultation, and training. These activities can support NATO operations both present (including those in Libya, Afghanistan, and Kosovo) and future. For example, Turkey routinely hosts the United States and other NATO militaries for Anatolian Falcon and (before its relationship worsened with Israel) Anatolian Eagle exercises held at its Konya air base in central Turkey. Other operations in which Turkey participates include, but are not limited to

- NATO's Operation Active Endeavor (a counterterrorism patrol in the Mediterranean Sea),
- a Standing NATO Maritime Group and a Standing NATO Response Force Mine Countermeasures Group,
- NATO's Baltic air policing mission, and

- the anti-piracy Combined Task Force 151 in the Gulf of Aden and off the coast of Somalia that involves several NATO member states.[98]

One measure of the utility of this U.S.-Turkey cooperation could be the level of joint participation and interoperability Turkey maintains with NATO in comparison with the levels maintained by other NATO allies. Another measure of the value of this cooperation could be the participation of Turkish armed forces in and the availability of Turkish bases for non-NATO training, exercises, and missions involving the United States or other NATO allies. Under the terms of the U.S.- Turkey DECA, Turkish governmental approval is required for the non-NATO U.S. use of Incirlik; other Turkish military installations; or Turkish territory, waters, and airspace for non-general training purposes. These purposes could include using joint-use bases or Turkish territory, waters, or airspace as staging grounds for military operations in the region—for which parliamentary approval is generally required.

Involving Non-NATO Militaries

As part of its efforts to diversify its relationships, Turkey has increasingly looked to countries outside of NATO for cooperation on military matters—from joint exercises and consultations to defense agreements. This includes Turkish cooperation with China,[99] Russia[100] (Turkey's primary energy import source), and countries in its surrounding region.[101] A sign that some analysts viewed as betokening further Turkish diversification from its Western relationships was Chinese participation in an air exercise with Turkey at Konya air base in September-October 2010 and in ground force exercises held in Turkey in November 2010.[102] Reportedly, Turkey used older F-4 fighter aircraft in the air exercise instead of more advanced F-16s to allay U.S. concerns about the possible transfer of technology to China.

CONCLUSION

The decades-long U.S.-Turkey defense relationship has passed through different phases during and after the Cold War. A confluence of developments over the past decade that include (1) the 2003 Iraq war and its consequences for U.S. influence in the region and the world, (2) greater Turkish engagement regionally and globally due to leadership from the ruling Justice and Development Party (AKP) and sustained economic growth, and (3) political change within Turkey that has reduced the military's influence and changed the tenor of public debate has contributed to a strategic environment in which divergences between U.S. and Turkish defense priorities and threat perceptions appear to many to carry greater implications than past divergences.

U.S. efforts to benefit from Turkey's location between the West and Middle East, both geographically and culturally/symbolically, may influence both U.S. and Turkish perceptions of the mutual benefits and leverage of the relationship. Some officials and analysts believe that in at least some respects the United States needs Turkey more than Turkey needs the United States, given (1) increased Turkish economic and military self-sufficiency, and (2) what they view as a relative decline of U.S. influence in the region and globally as other actors emerge—particularly those that have greater intimate knowledge of the region and more of an existential stake in its security.

Others counter that claims of Turkish leverage over the United States are exaggerated because

- Turkey's influence with the United States ultimately depends on its ability to help deliver regional outcomes that serve U.S. interests;
- the United States arguably can depend on other allies to deliver outcomes it desires; and
- it is unclear whether any potential non-NATO alliance could provide Turkey with superior, equal, or comparable (1) security guarantees, (2) regional influence and geopolitical prestige, or (3) collaborative benefits on military matters such as procurement, interoperability, or training.

Turkey may seek to use any leverage it has to take a more proactive role with its allies in shaping processes, outcomes, and institutional structures in response to changes it perceives in regional and international order.[103] These opportunities could increase in the wake of the political changes beginning in January 2011 that have affected the region, particularly Arab countries traditionally allied to the United States such as Egypt.

Current U.S.-Turkish defense cooperation, both bilaterally and within NATO, reflects shared interests in maintaining regional stability, manifested clearly through counterterrorism cooperation against the PKK in northern Iraq and Turkish participation in the ISAF mission in Afghanistan. Concerns about stability also motivate Turkey's agreement in principle to a NATO ballistic missile defense (BMD) system that anticipates potential threats from Iran. However, Turkey may not have yet decided whether it perceives hosting a proposed U.S. BMD radar under NATO auspices as, on balance, more likely to cultivate stability, or as unduly provocative to neighboring countries. Turkish estimations of the U.S. EPAA missile defense system's theoretical and practical capability to protect Turkish territory and populations would likely factor into a decision.

Mutual perceptions of the overall bilateral relationship—influenced by statements on Turkey's policies and rhetoric vis-à-vis Israel and Iran and possible action related to a potential Armenian genocide resolution by Members of Congress—may determine the extent of future U.S.-Turkey defense cooperation. The availability of Turkish bases and territory for U.S./NATO deployments, operations, and supply lines is valuable and remains a possible point of contention and leverage, but the extent of its importance and of alternatives may be subject to further analysis. The decline of the Turkish military's societal influence could affect the conduct of relations that have traditionally been largely managed between DOD and the Turkish General Staff. It also could affect the identity of key interlocutors on both sides, with possible consequences for the predictability to each side of the other's messaging, negotiating, and decision-making patterns.

Turkey's increasing diversification of defense contacts and potential procurement and industrial cooperation with non-NATO countries buttresses some analysts' assertions that it seeks greater autonomy and may be trending toward the more neutral international stance it adopted during the years between the founding of its republic in the 1920s and the beginning of the Cold War.[104] Although issues in the past year involving Turkey's stances on Israel and Iran have heightened the attention Westerners are paying to Turkey's strategic orientation, analysts such as Edward Erickson were discussing the issue as early as 2005:

> It is evident that the Turks do not want to be sidelined by the US or the West when it comes to their own national security concerns. Neither do they want to be hamstrung by easily severed logistics. Clearly they want to be, and have been thinking about becoming, important players in regional politics, and their public national security policy says as much. They have become involved at every opportunity in multi-national military interventions. They have shown a willingness to defy the US. They have industrial and procurement plans aimed at strategic autonomy.[105]

Yet, even given a more diversified and autonomous Turkish military production and procurement system, Turkey apparently covets various advanced military technologies—including fighter and drone aircraft, helicopters, and missile defense systems—for which the United States remains one of the only global suppliers. For the foreseeable future, the United States may be uniquely qualified to supply a wide range of arms to Turkey in light of Turkish objectives for military capability and interoperability.

Thus, despite changes to the U.S.-Turkey defense relationship, and the current lack of annual Foreign Military Financing funding, several factors indicate the importance for both countries of cooperating on a wide range issues that affect regional and global security. Without compromising its positions on core national security interests, Congress might take one or more general approaches on U.S.-Turkey defense cooperation (see "Possible U.S. Policy Approaches" above) both to minimize the frequency and scope of disagreement on security and procurement issues, and prevent the occasional differences on issues that do occur from disrupting common efforts on others or from harming the overall bilateral relationship or the NATO alliance.

Cold War Era

U.S.-Turkey defense cooperation began near the end of World War II when Turkey, having been neutral until February 1945, declared war on Germany and Japan to become a founding member of the United Nations. When it became clear after the war that Stalin's Soviet Union had designs on territory in eastern Turkey and on privileged naval access through Turkey's Bosporus and Dardanelles Straits to the Mediterranean, Turkey welcomed the April 1946 arrival of the U.S. battleship *U.S.S. Missouri* in Istanbul harbor. President Harry Truman's subsequent pledge in March 1947 of economic (Marshall Plan) and military assistance to both Turkey and Greece solidified Turkey's role as a Western ally and geographic buffer against Soviet influence. After Turkey's participation in United Nations forces during the Korean War gained it the reputation of a reliable and capable ally, Turkey joined NATO in 1952.

In subsequent years, the United States and Turkey signed military facilities and status of forces agreements, and the United States established more than 30 defense-related installations in Turkey with approximately 5,000 U.S. personnel, increasing to approximately 25,000 at the high point in the 1960s. In 1959, the United States stationed 15 Jupiter ballistic missiles with nuclear warheads in Turkey. These were removed as part of the U.S.-Soviet deal that ended the 1962 Cuban Missile Crisis, but were later replaced by tactical nuclear weapons, some of which reportedly remain in Turkey (see

Appendix A. Historical Overview

Chronology of Turkey-U.S. Defense Cooperation

1945	Turkey declares war on Germany and Japan in February; becomes founding member of the United Nations
1946	U.S.S. Missouri arrives in Istanbul Harbor in April
1947	President Harry Truman pledges economic (Marshall Plan) and military assistance to Turkey and Greece to counter Soviet influence
1950	Turkish forces join the United Nations contingent in the Korean War
1952	Turkey becomes a member of NATO
1954	United States and Turkey sign first status of forces agreement; U.S./NATO Cold War-era military presence established in Turkey
1960	Turkish military officers carry out first coup d'etat
1961	Deposed Prime Minister Adnan Menderes executed; new civilian government takes office following October elections
1962	Resolution of Cuban Missile Crisis includes U.S. agreement to remove Jupiter missiles with nuclear warheads from Turkey
1964	Letter from President Lyndon Johnson to Turkish Prime Minister Ismet Inonu (known as the "Johnson Letter") communicates U.S. opposition to Turkish intervention in Cyprus after Greek-Turkish power sharing had broken down
1971	Second coup d'etat by Turkish military in response to social and political turmoil
1973	Elective government reestablished
1974	Turkey sends troops using U.S.-supplied equipment to Cyprus on behalf of Turkish Cypriot minority
1975	Congress imposes arms embargo on Turkey for its actions in Cyprus
	Turkey abrogates U.S. status of forces agreement; takes control of U.S. installations; U.S. forces performing NATO functions remain
1978	U.S. arms embargo on Turkey ends
1980	U.S.-Turkey Defense and Economic Cooperation Agreement signed—U.S. military presence on Turkish installations is under NATO auspices
	Third coup d'etat by Turkish military in response to social and political turmoil
	Turgut Ozal, Deputy Prime Minister for Economic Affairs, accelerates economic liberalization and reform under military rule
1982	New Turkish constitution ratified
1983	Turgut Ozal becomes prime minister of new civilian government; economic liberalization and reform continue
1984	PKK armed insurgency begins in southeastern Turkey
1990-1991	Turkey joins coalition effort against Iraq in Gulf War; allows U.S. use of bases for air strikes; closes Iraq-Turkey oil pipeline and amasses troops on border with Iraq
	U.S.-British air forces continue to use Turkish bases to patrol northern Iraq following Gulf War
1992	Treaty on Conventional Armed Forces in Europe (CFE Treaty) enters into force as Cold War ends
	Major U.S. military grant aid to Turkey discontinued in post-Cold War environment
1997	Turkish coalition government led by Islamist Welfare (Refah) Party resigns under pressure from Turkish military

Appendix A. (Continued)

1999	Turkey captures PKK leader Abdullah Ocalan; PKK declares cease-fire
2001	Al Qaeda stages multiple attacks in United States on September 11
	Turkey enacts International Monetary Fund-mandated anti-inflation reforms
2002	Justice and Development Party (AKP, a Welfare Party offshoot) wins majority in Turkish Grand National Assembly (Parliament)
2003	Recep Tayyip Erdogan becomes prime minister
	Turkish Parliament refuses to allow U.S. invasion of Iraq from Turkey; allows U.S. use of Turkish bases for overflight of Iraq after U.S.-led occupation of Iraq
	"Hood incident" involving U.S. military detainment of Turkish special forces troops occurs in Suleimaniyah, Iraq, negatively affecting Turkish public opinion toward the United States
2004	PKK cease-fire ends; PKK resumes insurgency and terrorist attacks against Turkey from safe havens in northern Iraq
2007	AKP parliamentary majority reelected; AKP's Abdullah Gul (former prime minister and foreign minister) elected president of Turkey
	U.S. begins close military and intelligence cooperation with Turkey against PKK in northern Iraq
2009	Ahmet Davutoglu becomes foreign minister
2010	Mavi Marmara flotilla incident severely damages already-worsening Turkey-Israel relations
	Turkey and Brazil joint declaration on possible nuclear fuel swaps with Iran; shortly thereafter, both countries cast the only "no" votes on U.N. Security Council Resolution 1929, which establishes enhanced sanctions against Iran
	Constitutional amendments approved in nationwide referendum, increasing civilian control over the military and judiciary
	United States, Turkey, and their NATO allies agree to territorial and population missile defense as an alliance-wide mission
2011	United States, Turkey, and their NATO allies agree to take over military operations in Libya aimed at implementing U.N. Security Council Resolution 1973 ("Operation Unified Protector"), with aerial mission commanded from Allied Air Component Command in Izmir

"Bases and Transport Corridors"). In addition, the United States provided Turkey with more than $4.5 billion in military assistance from 1948 to 1975—an average of approximately $160 million per year—to help it man, equip, train, and modernize its armed forces.

The U.S.-Turkey defense relationship endured complications during the Cold War. Cyprus was a major source of those troubles, particularly in the 1960s and 1970s. A strongly-worded letter from President Lyndon Johnson to Turkish Prime Minister Ismet Inonu may have helped prevent Turkish intervention on the island in 1964 following the breakdown of Greek-Turkish power sharing, but it raised questions about how well the U.S. alliance served Turkey's interests that intensified greatly when Turkey sent troops using U.S.-supplied arms to intervene on behalf of the Turkish Cypriot minority in 1974 and Congress responded with the 1975-1978 embargo on U.S. military grants and arms sales to Turkey described in the main body of the report (see "Background").

Although the alliance revived in 1980 with a new Defense and Economic Cooperation Agreement (DECA) in the wake of the Soviet invasion of Afghanistan and the Iranian Revolution, Turkey emphasized that the U.S. military presence on Turkish installations was under NATO auspices. U.S. military assistance was restored as well, reaching unprecedented levels in historical terms with an approximate annual average of $425 million in grants and $110 million in loans from 1987 to 1992. This facilitated a general upgrade of Turkey's weapons systems. Post-1980 U.S. military assistance to Greece and Turkey was provided at a 7-to-10 ratio. Although Turkey received the greater amount, it routinely complained that its size, share of NATO's military burden, and relative importance to Western interests justified an even greater proportional advantage over Greece.

As the Cold War was ending, Turkey joined its NATO allies and the Warsaw Pact countries, including the United States and the Soviet Union, in entering into the Treaty on Conventional Armed Forces in Europe (CFE Treaty). The CFE Treaty sought to maintain peace and stability among former Cold War adversaries by limiting types and levels of conventional forces, both Europe-wide and in certain key regions (which included Turkey), and subjecting the parties to joint monitoring. The treaty was signed in 1990 and entered into force in 1992. Russia, however, unilaterally suspended its compliance in 2007, partly due to lingering disagreements with other parties over its force posture in sensitive "flank zones"—including areas opposite the northeastern Turkish border in Georgia and in Russia's North Caucasian periphery.[106]

Post-Cold War Era: Two Iraq Wars

For the 1991 Gulf War, Turkey allowed the U.S.-led coalition to use its bases for air strikes on Iraqi territory after closing a pipeline through which Iraq had exported oil through Turkish territory. Also, the amassing of troops by Turkey on Iraq's northern border helped the coalition's efforts by drawing significant Iraqi troop strength away from the southern front in the Gulf from which the invasion came. Nevertheless, the run-up to the war presaged future subjections of the military to strong civilian leadership when then-Chief of the Turkish General Staff, General Necip Torumtay, resigned out of disagreement with then-President Turgut Ozal's decision to involve Turkey in the war.[107] In the war's aftermath, U.S. and British military aircraft based at Turkey's Incirlik air base patrolled the no-fly zone established at the end of hostilities in the heavily Kurdish-populated areas of northern Iraq. Although the Gulf War had reinforced Turkey's geostrategic importance to the United States and NATO, the end of the Cold War appeared to Congress to have removed the rationale for providing large amounts of grant aid to arm the Turkish military. Foreign Military Financing (FMF) grants were phased into loan-only assistance in 1993, and the loans were phased out after 1997.

In the aftermath of the Al Qaeda terrorist attacks of September 11, 2001, on U.S. territory, Turkey gained new importance as a possible staging ground for U.S.-led military action in the region. Given that Turkey had allowed the United States use of its air bases for limited military action in Iraq since 1991, and had subsequently participated with the United States in missions in Somalia, Bosnia-Herzegovina, Kosovo, and Afghanistan, George W. Bush Administration officials believed they could obtain permission to station U.S. ground troops at Turkey's border with Iraq to open a second front in the 2003 Iraq war. After the newly elected government led by the Islamic-leaning Justice and Development Party (AKP) secured promises of approximately $24 billion in U.S. aid and loan guarantees (including $15 billion in immediate aid), it overcame its initial reservations to agree, albeit somewhat lukewarmly, to the U.S. plan. However, the Turkish Parliament failed to muster the absolute majority (based on the total amount of parliamentary votes possible) required to approve the U.S. request in March 2003 (even though "yes" votes outnumbered "no" votes 264-251) when nearly 100 AKP members voted against the measure or abstained, possibly due to an unwillingness to endorse invading a fellow Muslim country. This surprise, which forced the Bush Administration into last-minute adjustments for a single front, led to serious U.S. displeasure with its Turkish ally.

Analysts have advanced several possible explanations for the Turkish Parliament's 2003 decision on Iraq. One is that the United States, in its request to stage a ground invasion from Turkey, asked for *more* in 2003 than it did in 1991, even though many believed that the U.S. argument for going to war against Iraq was *less* merited, and the threat Saddam Hussein posed to Turkey *less* severe.

Another is that the benefits Turkey received for its cooperation in the 1991 war were significantly fewer than expected, leading Turkish lawmakers to reduce expectations in their cost-benefit analysis for 2003. Many were skeptical that U.S. and other international aid (particularly from Gulf states)

Turkey received for its support in 1991—though substantial (approximately $17 billion in arms and military and economic aid)[108]—had been worth the costs incurred in (1) reduced trade from the war and from international sanctions against Iraq (estimated at between $30 billion-$60 billion)[109], (2) regional destabilization and refugee influxes, and (3) the emboldening of Kurdish separatists (especially the PKK) to operate from greater safe haven in northern Iraq. Turkey's hopes in 1990-1991 that its cooperation might decisively cement its economic, political, and security integration with Europe had been frustrated by NATO's tepid response (reprised during the run-up to the 2003 war) in committing in advance of the war to the collective defense of Turkey under Article 5 in the event of an Iraqi attack, as well as by continued uncertainty over Turkey's European Union (EU) membership prospects.

In addition, strides Turkey had made since the 1991 war to increase its economic and military self-sufficiency and to reduce threats on its borders contributed to perceptions that it was less dependent on U.S. assistance.[110] A 2007 *Turkish Studies* article said,

> In the end, it appears that the Turks' appraisal of the strength of their position *vis-à-vis* the United States was accurate. Despite Turkey's refusal to facilitate the invasion, the United States went to significant lengths to make sure Turkey's vital interests were looked after. Not only did the United States not change its position on Kurdish independence and continued to push for a democratic, centralized regime in Iraq, but the United States even ... reinstated Turkey as a recipient of regular financial aid. The reason for this American generosity is that in the end, while very disappointed about the way relations had soured, US officials realized that they did not want to cause Turkish decisionmakers to reconsider their fundamental alignment.[111]

Nevertheless, as mentioned in the main body of the report (see "Background") the Turkish Parliament's 2003 decision on Iraq showed the United States that in its defense relationship with Turkey, it could no longer rely solely on past legacies of cooperation and its close ties with the Turkish military.

Ultimately, Turkey allowed U.S. overflights into Iraq, and after the United States coalition had occupied Iraq and begun stability, counterinsurgency, and reconstruction operations, Turkey permitted the United States use of Turkish bases and border crossings for troop rotations and transport of non-lethal cargo to and from Iraq. The resumption of PKK attacks in Turkey following the U.S.-led invasion in 2003, however, has made countering terrorism from the

PKK's northern Iraqi safe havens a core Turkish security concern that has led to further U.S.-Turkey tensions. Since late 2007, Turkey has received direct U.S. cooperation in countering the PKK, and it reportedly seeks to acquire more advanced equipment to increase its own counterterrorism capabilities.

As mentioned above, the United States resumed FMF grant assistance to Turkey after September 11, 2001, averaging $27 million per year from 2002 to 2007. This assistance was completely phased out once more in FY2010, leaving International Military Education and Training (IMET), International Narcotics Control and Law Enforcement (INCLE), and Nonproliferation, Antiterrorism, Demining, and Related Programs (NADR) funds as the primary sources of annual U.S. military and security assistance to Turkey. DOD holds approximately $75 million of unobligated FMF funds appropriated for Turkey in prior years in reserve for potential future use (see "Military and Security Assistance").

APPENDIX B. TURKISH PROCUREMENT AND DEFENSE INDUSTRY POLICY

Turkey and the United States have a history of defense industry cooperation. Traditionally, many U.S. aircraft Turkey has purchased have been assembled in Turkey by TUSAS Aerospace Industries, which was partially owned by U.S.-based companies Lockheed Martin and General Electric International. This helped Turkey develop an indigenous defense industry that is becoming a major supplier in its surrounding region. For example, Turkey has since assembled 46 F-16s for Egypt and upgraded dozens more for Jordan.[112]

In 2005, state-owned Turkish Aircraft Industries bought out the remaining TUSAS shares and formed Turkish Aerospace Industries (TAI) through a merger, signifying an increasing emphasis by the state on boosting its indigenous defense production capacity.

Other major Turkish defense firms include (1) Aselsan, which specializes in electronics and software; (2) Roketsan, which specializes in missile technology; and (3) Otokar, which specializes in land-based vehicles. As noted in Figure 2, Turkey's procurement objectives called for 50% indigenous defense production by the end of 2010, and Foreign Trade Minister Zefer Caglayan claimed in August 2010 that indigenous production reached 46% in 2009. The strategic plan also calls for at least a 50% return in direct or indirect offsets on procurement agreements with a value of at least $10 million.

Emphasis on procurement from countries and firms that provide offsets, allow co-production, and issue export licenses at the bidding stage can be at odds with U.S. arms export laws and practices, particularly when sensitive technology is involved, and has made it more difficult for U.S. firms to obtain contracts.

Thus, as mentioned in "Arms Sales and Industrial Cooperation," Turkey looks to other suppliers that may not be as technologically advanced or reliable, but that Turkey perceives as being more flexible in negotiations and in sharing expertise, and therefore more helpful in contributing to Turkey's long-term goal of industrial self-reliance. The following are some examples of recent or pending Turkish defense procurement tenders:[113]

- *Attack Helicopters.* In 2007, Turkey chose to purchase 50 "T129" variants of the A129 Mangusta attack and tactical reconnaissance (ATAK) helicopter (with an option for another 41) for $2.7 billion. Although Italy's AgustaWestland is the main technology source, TAI is designated as the primary contractor to cultivate the image of Turkish self-reliance. A prominent Turkish procurement official had voiced a preference for off-the-shelf U.S. Apache or Cobra helicopters, and U.S. officials claimed that the bidding process unfairly excluded U.S. firms. When the test aircraft crashed in 2010, likely pushing delivery beyond the planned 2013 date, Turkey sought to acquire U.S. Bell AH-1W SuperCobras as a stopgap measure. When the United States told Turkey it was unable to meet Turkey's timeline for the stopgap delivery, Turkey purchased nine Mangustas from AgustaWestland for $209 million, with delivery slated for 2012 after TAI assembles the exported kits. U.S. firms will provide the helicopter engines in any case.[114]
- *Utility Helicopters.* U.S. firm Sikorsky Aircraft is competing with AgustaWestland to sell Turkey 109 utility helicopters for approximately $4 billion, with the possibility of selling nearly 200 more in the future. As is the case regarding Turkey's attack helicopter deal with AgustaWestland, TAI would be listed as the prime contractor and would co-produce the utility helicopters, which would replace Turkey's aging fleet dominated by U.S.-exported Black Hawks and Hueys. Both Sikorsky (which is offering a Turkish version of its S-70 Black Hawk International) and AgustaWestland (offering a Turkish version of its A149) have offered several extras to make their offers more attractive, focusing on offsets and opportunities for Turkish

export production. Turkey's Defense Industry Executive Committee may make a decision on the tender as early as March 2011.

- *Cargo Transport Aircraft.* Turkey joined a consortium with six European NATO allies in 2001 for the Airbus A400M transport plane, and plans to purchase 10. The program has been delayed and experienced cost overruns, but the consortium reportedly signed a final contract in April 2011.[115] In the meantime, Saudi Arabia has agreed to sell Turkey six older model U.S.-origin C-130s to meet Turkey's interim needs,[116] pending congressional notification.
- *Battle Tanks.* In July 2008, South Korea's Hyundai Rotem signed a $400 million contract with Turkish company Otokar to develop and produce up to 250 main battle tanks. Under the terms of the deal, Hyundai Rotem will supply more than 50% of the technology to develop the tanks and will work alongside Otokar on the design and development of four prototypes.
- *Anti-Tank Missile Systems.* Russia's Rosoboronexport agreed to deliver about 800 Kornet-E medium-range anti-tank missile systems to Turkey for $100 million as a stopgap measure while Turkish firm Roketsan continues to develop an indigenous medium-range anti-tank missile system.
- *Submarines.* Turkey will acquire six Type 214 submarines (to replace some of its 1970s-era Atilay-class Type 209 submarines) from Germany's HowaldtswerkeDeutsche Werft (HDW, Turkey's longtime submarine supplier) and its United Kingdom-based commercial partner MarineForce International (MFI) under a $3.96 billion contract signed in July 2009, with delivery expected between 2015 and 2020. Turkish Minister of National Defense Vecdi Gonul said in July 2008 that Turkish industrial participation is expected to reach about 80% of the contract, with approximately 20 systems and subsystems produced and integrated locally.

Aspirations for indigenous Turkish defense industrial capabilities extend to large drone aircraft[117] (Turkey already produces small drones for deployment) and missile defense systems, but current Turkish plans indicate that in the near term, Turkey seeks to acquire this equipment and possibly share in its assembly in the hopes that it may receive technology and develop a knowledge base and infrastructure that shortens the timeline for indigenous design and production.

As it begins to meet its own security demands and develops higher quantities of more advanced equipment, external demand for Turkish arms has led to increased exports. According to Jane's World Defence Industry,

> To date, Turkish industries have exported only eight platforms: among these are missiles, rocket launchers, radios, tracked and wheeled vehicles, electronic systems, pilot simulators and coastguard craft.
>
> The electronic systems and pilot simulators alone represent "big ticket" items that can generate the necessary income for Turkey's indigenous industries to develop not only the production base but also the Research and Development (R&D) institutions necessary for large-scale expansion.
>
> The SSM [Defense Procurement Undersecretariat] has highlighted the Netherlands, Pakistan, the United Arab Emirates, South Korea, Algeria and Bahrain as recent destinations for Turkish defence materiel.
>
> In addition, in June 2008, Turkey's Foreign Trade Minister, Kursad Tuzmen, highlighted the Asia Pacific region as a potential target region for defence sales.[118]

Nevertheless, according to the Stockholm International Peace Research Institute, in 2009 Turkey was the world's 10th largest arms importer and only its 26th largest exporter.

As noted in Figure 2, a promotional office affiliated with Turkey's procurement agency, the SSM, opened near Washington, DC, in 2010, and similar offices are planned to open soon in Europe (Belgium), the Persian Gulf (Qatar), and the Caucasus and Central Asia (either Azerbaijan or Turkmenistan).

End Notes

[1] Henri J. Barkey, "Turkey's New Global Role," Carnegie Endowment for International Peace, November 17, 2010, available at http://carnegieendowment.org/publications /?fa=view &id=41952. The challenge for U.S. officials to manage cooperation with Turkey could be magnified by the way the U.S. government is structured to work with Turkey. Former U.S. ambassador to Turkey Mark Parris has said, "For reasons of self-definition and Cold War logic, Turkey is considered a European nation. It is therefore assigned, for purposes of policy development and implementation, to the subdivisions responsible for Europe: the European Bureau (EUR) at the State Department; the European Command (EUCOM) at the Pentagon; the Directorate for Europe at the [National Security Council (NSC)], etc. Since the end of the Cold War, however, and progressively since the 1990-91 Gulf War and 9/11, the most serious issues in U.S.-Turkish relations – and virtually all of the controversial ones – have arisen in areas outside "Europe." The majority, in fact, stem from developments in

areas which in Washington are the responsibility of offices dealing with the Middle East: the Bureau for Near East Affairs (NEA) at State; Central Command (CENTCOM) at the Pentagon; the Near East and South Asia Directorate at NSC." Omer Taspinar, "The Rise of Turkish Gaullism: Getting Turkish-American Relations Right," *Insight Turkey*, vol. 13, no. 1, winter 2011, quoting an unpublished 2008 paper by Mark Parris.

[2] Morton Abramowitz, a former U.S. ambassador to Turkey, provided an analysis of the issue in a March 19, 2010 article for *nationalinterest.org* entitled "The Never-Ending Armenian Genocide Resolution."

[3] Andrew Mango, *The Turks Today* (New York: The Overlook Press, 2004), p. 62.

[4] See, e.g., Foreign Assistance Act (P.L. 93-559) for FY1975 enacted December 30, 1974. No similar measures were taken against Greece, even though its troops also used U.S. equipment in Cyprus.

[5] Aylin Guney, "An Anatomy of the Transformation of the US-Turkish Alliance: From 'Cold War' to 'War on Iraq,'" *Turkish Studies*, vol. 6, no. 3, September 2005.

[6] Barkey, op. cit.

[7] Sevil Kucukkosum, "Turks see U.S. as biggest external threat, poll results show," *Hurriyet Daily News & Economic Review*, January 5, 2011. The poll, taken by the MetroPOLL Strategic and Social Research Center, which is affiliated with Turkey's ruling Justice and Development Party (AKP), stated that 43% of respondents viewed the United States as Turkey's primary external threat, with Israel in second place with 24%. Iran was a distant third with 3%. Ibid.

[8] Although it received little enduring attention in the United States, the so-called "hood incident" connected with the 2003 Iraq war exacerbated popular Turkish opposition to the U.S. invasion. On July 4, 2003, U.S. soldiers captured approximately 11 Turkish special forces soldiers during a raid on a safehouse in the northern Iraqi city of Suleimaniyah. Those captured were under suspicion for involvement in a plot to assassinate the Kurdish governor of Kirkuk province. After their arrest, the Turkish soldiers had hoods put over their heads and were interrogated before Turkish military and diplomatic protestations led to their release 60 hours later. Since the 1990s, there had been reports of Turkish special forces units operating in northern Iraq and allying themselves with an Iraqi Turkomen militia to monitor and operate against the PKK. See "A partnership at risk?", *Economist*, July 10, 2003. Though neither side apologized for its part in the hood incident, both issued statements of regret. The resumption of PKK attacks on targets in Turkey following the Iraq invasion led to Turkish perceptions that the United States was insufficiently aware of or concerned about the difficulties these attacks present to Turkey.

[9] See Kucukkosum, op. cit.

[10] BBC World Service Poll, "Views of US Continue to Improve in 2011 BBC Country Rating Poll," March 7, 2011, available at http://www.worldpublicopinion.org /pipa/pdf /mar11 /BBCEvalsUS_Mar11_rpt.pdf. The poll, which was conducted from December 2010 to February 2011, claimed that 35% of Turks believe that U.S. influence in the world is positive (up from 13% in 2010), and that 49% believe that U.S. influence is negative (down from 68% in 2010).

[11] The National Intelligence Council reported in 2008 that "Turkey's recent economic track record of increased growth, the vitality of Turkey's emerging middle class and its geostrategic locale raise the prospect of a growing regional role in the Middle East." U.S. National Intelligence Council, *Global Trends 2025: A Transformed World*, November 2008, available at http://www.dni.gov/nic/PDF_2025/2025_Global_Trends_Final_Report.pdf.

[12] For a discussion and maps of various existing and proposed pipelines and energy transit routes through and near Turkey, see Transatlantic Academy, *Getting to Zero: Turkey, Its Neighbors, and the West*, June 2010, available at http://www.transatlanticacademy.org /sites/default/files/publications/GettingtoZeroFINAL.pdf.

[13] See, e.g., "Great sacrifices, small rewards," *Economist*, December 29, 2010.

[14] See Gareth Jenkins, "On the edge – The AKP shifts Turkey's political compass," *Jane's Intelligence Review*, August 2, 2010.

[15] See CRS Report RL34642, *Turkey: Selected Foreign Policy Issues and U.S. Views*, by Jim Zanotti.

[16] Robert Tait and Ewen McCaskill, "Turkey threatens 'serious consequences' after US vote on Armenian genocide," *Guardian* (UK), March 5, 2010.

[17] See CRS Report R41275, *Israel's Blockade of Gaza, the Mavi Marmara Incident, and Its Aftermath*, by Carol Migdalovitz.

[18] "US official: Turkey must demonstrate commitment to West," *Today's Zaman*, June 28, 2010.

[19] Ercan Yavuz, "Israeli-caused instability makes its way to Turkey's security document," *Today's Zaman*, October 29, 2010.

[20] See CRS Report RL34642, *Turkey: Selected Foreign Policy Issues and U.S. Views*, by Jim Zanotti.

[21] Daniel Dombey, "US issues arms-deal ultimatum to Turkey," *Financial Times*, August 15, 2010.

[22] See, e.g., Ariel Cohen, "Congressmen Talk Turkey," Heritage Foundation, June 21, 2010, available at http://blog.heritage.org/?p=36681.

[23] The proposed elements of the EPAA and a deployment timeline are described in a September 17, 2009 White House press release available at http://www.whitehouse.gov /the_press_office/FACT-SHEET-US-Missile-Defense-Policy-APhased-Adaptive-Approach-for-Missile-Defense-in-Europe/. See also CRS Report R41549, *Missile Defense and NATO's Lisbon Summit*, by Steven A. Hildreth and Carl Ek.

[24] Marc Champion, "Turkey in Dilemma Over NATO Shield," *Wall Street Journal*, October 27, 2010.

[25] NATO Lisbon Summit Declaration, November 20, 2010, available at http://www.nato.int /cps/en/natolive/ official_texts_68828.htm?mode=pressrelease.

[26] Louis Charbonneau, "EXCLUSIVE-Turkey says seizes illegal Iran arms shipment," *Reuters*, March 31, 2011. According to this article, the cache included 60 Kalashnikov AK-47 assault rifles, 14 BKC/Bixi machine guns, nearly 8,000 rounds of BKC/AK-47 ammunition, 560 60-mm mortar shells, and 1,288 120-mm mortar shells. Ibid.

[27] In addition to authorizing the enforcement of a no-fly zone over Libya, Resolution 1973 authorized all U.N. countries, "acting nationally or through regional organizations or arrangements ... to take all necessary measures ... to protect civilians and civilian populated areas under threat of attack in the Libyan Arab Jamahiriya, including Benghazi, while excluding a foreign occupation force of any form on any part of Libyan territory".

[28] See Ipek Yezdani, "Turkey seeks ways to stay in NATO game," *Hurriyet Daily News & Economic Review*, March 24, 2011.

[29] "Wary of France, Turkey Wants NATO in Charge of Libya," *Today's Zaman*, March 25, 2011. Turkish officials objected vociferously to what they perceived as an overly aggressive stance from France. They were clearly displeased with being excluded from the U.S.-U.K.-France meetings in Paris that preceded the initial coalition air strikes. France explained that Turkey had been excluded because of Erdogan's previous statements of opposition to military intervention and to a NATO role in Libya. Many media reports have painted the

subsequent NATO deliberations as largely a contest between France, which favored a coalition possibly outside NATO command and freer rein to take offensive action; and Turkey, which, like the United States, favored having NATO control the entire operation. France-Turkey tensions owe much to France's leading role in opposing full EU membership for Turkey.

[30] The principle of consensus or unanimity that governs NATO gives each ally virtual veto power over the alliance's political and military decisions.

[31] "Turkey to assume control of Benghazi airport in Libya," *Hurriyet Daily News & Economic Review*, March 28, 2011.

[32] For more information on the NATO-led operation, see CRS Report R41725, *Operation Odyssey Dawn (Libya): Background and Issues for Congress*, coordinated by Jeremiah Gertler.

[33] Burak Ege Bekdil and Umit Enginsoy, "Turkey to Have Triple Role in Libya Mission," *Defense News*, March 29, 2011.

[34] According to the blog, "Erdogan reportedly told Rasmussen that NATO's Izmir base could only be closed after Turkey becomes a European Union member, claiming that the base is the single component that maintains Turkey's links with trans-Atlantic space." Jorge Benitez, "Rasmussen fails to persuade Turkey to close Izmir base," *acus.org/natosource,* April 7, 2011.

[35] The Ataturk-led Turkish army was responsible for driving out invading European powers following the end of World War I to prevent the partition of the core Ottoman lands of Eastern Thrace and Anatolia.

[36] In 1997, the military did not directly overthrow the government, but in what has been called a "post-modern" coup, compelled the dissolution of the first-ever Islamist-led coalition government in the wake of manifestations of public Islamist sentiment. In the years following the collapse of the government, junior members of the former coalition-leading Islamist party (former Prime Minister Necmettin Erbakan's Refah (Welfare) Party), including Recep Tayyip Erdogan and Abdullah Gul, formed the currently ruling Justice and Development Party (AKP), which they have characterized since the AKP's inception as a center-right reformist party without an Islamist agenda.

[37] Gareth Jenkins, *Context and Circumstance: The Turkish Military and Politics*, International Institute for Strategic Studies, Adelphi Paper 337, Oxford University Press, New York, 2001.

[38] According to Steven Cook of the Council on Foreign Relations: "The most important changes were made to the National Security Council (known more commonly by its Turkish acronym, MGK), which had been the primary channel through which the officers influenced Turkish politics." Steven A. Cook, "The Weakening of Turkey's Military," Council on Foreign Relations Expert Brief, March 1, 2010, available at http://www.cfr.org/publication/21548/weakening_ofjurkeys_military.html.

[39] The AKP's popularity in 2007 elections could be seen as a combination of multiple factors, among which could be (1) the significant and sustained economic growth that most analysts believe was partly facilitated by International Monetary Fund-mandated anti-inflation reforms enacted in 2001 (the year before it came to power), (2) general support for the AKP's policy and reform agenda, and (3) the lack of a compelling or coherent opposition.

[40] "Balance of power," *Economist*, October 21, 2010.

[41] "Armed Forces, Turkey," op. cit.

[42] Ismet Akca, *Military-Economic Structure in Turkey: Present Situation, Problems, and Solutions*. Turkish Economic and Social Studies Foundation (TESEV) Publications, July 2010, available at http://www.tesev.org.tr/UD_OBJS/PDF/ DEMP/ENG/gsr-2-eng.pdf.

[43] 32 U.S.T. 3323; TIAS 9901.

[44] See Saban Kardas, "Davutoglu Outlines the Contours of the New Turkish Foreign Policy," *Eurasia Daily Monitor*, Vol. 8, No. 4, January 6, 2011, available at http://www.jamestown.org/single/?no_cache=1& tx_ttnews[tt_news]=37326.

[45] See, e.g., German Marshall Fund of the United States, *Transatlantic Trends: Key Findings 2009*, available at http://trends.gmfus.org/doc/2009_English_Key.pdf. This report summarized polling results that reflected differences in attitudes toward NATO and various security-related issues between Turks and citizens of other NATO countries. See also Umit Enginsoy, "Turkey still the outlier as world mulls no-fly zone over Libya," *Hurriyet Daily News & Economic Review*, March 1, 2011.

[46] The Turkish and Greek foreign ministries both provide information on the Aegean dispute, which centers on territorial issues over islands, waters, and airspace. See http://www.mfa.gov.tr/background-note-on-aegeandispute.en.mfa; and http://www.mfa.gr /www.mfa.gr/en-US/Policy/Geographic+Regions/South-Eastern+Europe/ Turkey/.

[47] Article 5 of The North Atlantic Treaty (NATO's founding and governing charter) reads: "The Parties agree that an armed attack against one or more of them in Europe or North America shall be considered an attack against them all and consequently they agree that, if such an armed attack occurs, each of them, in exercise of the right of individual or collective self-defence recognised by Article 51 of the Charter of the United Nations, will assist the Party or Parties so attacked by taking forthwith, individually and in concert with the other Parties, such action as it deems necessary, including the use of armed force, to restore and maintain the security of the North Atlantic area."

[48] "US Defence Secretary Gates blames EU for Turkey 'drift,'" *BBC News*, June 9, 2010.

[49] Ardan Zenturk, "They Brought Disarray to Libya; We Are Tidying Up," *Star Online* (Istanbul) (translated from Turkish), March 24, 2011, Open Source Document GMP20110324016020.

[50] Umit Enginsoy and Burak Ege Bekdil, "Libya Crisis Widens Turk-West Differences," *Defense News*, March 21, 2011.

[51] Sevil Kucukkosum, "Missile diplomacy latest test for US-NATO-Turk ties," *Hurriyet Daily News & Economic Review*, October 21, 2010.

[52] Champion, op. cit.

[53] Ian O. Lesser, "Turkey, the NATO Summit, and After," German Marshall Fund of the United States "On Turkey" Analysis, November 23, 2010, available at http://www.gmfus.org /galleries/ct_publication_attachments/Lesser_NATO_Nov10.pdf;jsessionid=aux1Dml-YRNcrd6jJZ.

[54] See, e.g., U.S.-Turkey memorandum of understanding for a bilateral missile defense architecture analysis, June 6, 2001, available at http://turkey.usembassy.gov/treaty_pdf /ctia10089.pdf.

[55] See footnote 70.

[56] A March/April 2011 article in *The Bulletin of the Atomic Scientists* stated that Turkey sees tactical nuclear weapons based on its territory as "playing an important security role, providing reassurance of American assistance in the event of an emergency and a 'hook' tethering Turkey to the European mainland. The nuclear weapons also appear to perform a nonproliferation function: As long as Turkey has access to US nuclear weapons it can turn to in extremis, there is no need for Ankara to consider developing its own nuclear weapons option." Mark Fitzpatrick, "How Europeans view tactical nuclear weapons on their

continent," *The Bulletin of the Atomic Scientists*, vol. 67, no. 2, March/April 2011. Nevertheless, in light of advocacy begun in 2010 by Germany, the Netherlands, Belgium, (three of the four other states where U.S. tactical nuclear weapons are reportedly stationed under NATO auspices—Italy is the fourth), Norway, and Luxembourg for the removal of the approximately 150-200 U.S. tactical nuclear weapons from European territory, and in light of prospects within the next year for U.S.-Russia negotiations on curtailing tactical nuclear weapons in Europe (Russia reportedly has approximately 2,000), some analysts doubt that Turkey would contest the weapons' removal from its territory. Turkish analyst and former diplomat Sinan Ulgen has noted that "The question of denuclearization has not been politicized in Turkey." Rachel Oswald, "Polish, Turkish Experts Open to U.S. Withdrawing Nukes from Europe," *Global Security Newswire*, March 31, 2011.

[57] Craig Whitlock, "NATO near adoption of US missile shield," *Washington Post*, October 15, 2010.

[58] See Lesser, op cit.

[59] Information dated January 2011 provided to CRS by Turkish Embassy in Washington, DC.

[60] For further discussion of this question, see "Turkey's Importance to U.S. National Security" above.

[61] Anthony Shadid, "Resurgent Turkey Flexes Its Muscles Around Iraq," *New York Times*, January 4, 2011.

[62] Transcript of speech by U.S. Lt. Gen. Michael D. Barbero, Commander of NATO Training Mission-Iraq, Ankara, Turkey, October 2010, available at http://www.aco.nato.int/page12822541.aspx.

[63] U.S. State Department, *Country Reports on Terrorism 2009*, Chapter 6. Terrorist Organizations, August 2010, available at http://www.state.gov/s/ct/rls/crt/2009/140900.htm.

[64] Project Ploughshares, *Armed Conflicts Report 2010*, Turkey, available at http://www.ploughshares.ca/libraries/ACRText/ACR-Turkey2.htm. Between 2,300 and 2,500 are estimated to have been killed since 2003. A *Los Angeles Times* blog estimated that of the casualties since the beginning of the conflict, some 5,000 Turks and some 35,000 Kurds have died. Becky Lee Katz, "TURKEY: Kurdish teenager convicted as terrorist for attending demonstration," *latimes.com*, July 19, 2010.

[65] U.S. State Department, *2009 Country Reports on Human Rights Practices*, Turkey, March 11, 2010, available at http://www.state.gov/g/drl/rls/hrrpt/2009/eur/136062.htm.

[66] *Country Reports on Terrorism 2009*, op. cit.

[67] This had followed previous situations in 2006 and 2007 in which Turkey made similar mobilizations in the border area and the Bush Administration appointed retired General Joseph Ralston, former Supreme Allied Commander Europe, as U.S. Special Envoy for Countering the PKK. Ralston served in this position until October 2007.

[68] Ann Scott Tyson and Robin Wright, "U.S. Helps Turkey Hit Rebel Kurds in Iraq," *Washington Post*, December 18, 2007.

[69] "Armed Forces, Turkey," op. cit.

[70] Robert S. Norris and Hans M. Kristensen, "US tactical nuclear weapons in Europe, 2011," *The Bulletin of the Atomic Scientists*, vol. 67, no. 1, January/February 2011. Reportedly, the U.S. has approximately 150-200 B61 bombs in Turkey, Belgium, Germany, Italy, and the Netherlands left over from their deployment during the Cold War. This amount is a very small fraction of the over 7,000 U.S. tactical nuclear weapons stationed in Europe during the 1970s. Ibid.

[71] The Partnership for Peace Training Center (http://www.bioem.tsk.tr/) offers defense and security-related education and training opportunities for representatives from countries that

are members of NATO or NATO's Partnership for Peace (PfP), Mediterranean Dialogue (MD), or Istanbul Cooperation Initiative (ICI). Information on the PfP, MD, and ICI and participating countries can be found at http://www.nato.int/cps/en/natolive /topics_50349.htm and http://www.nato.int/cps/en/natolive/topics_59419.htm?.

[72] NATO's Center for Excellence-Defense Against Terrorism (http://www.coedat.nato.int/) offers a wide range of counterterrorism-related education and training opportunities. 27 NATO countries have participated, along with 77 other countries.

[73] Taspinar, op. cit.

[74] See, e.g., Scott A. Field and Dariush Zahedi, "The U.S. Security Strategy and the Role of Turkey in the New Middle East," *Turkish Policy Quarterly*, vol. 9, no. 3, December 2010, available at http://www.turkishpolicy.com/dosyalar/ files/71-82.pdf.

[75] For an argument that appears to support this position, see Robert Wexler, "United States and Turkey: Allies at Odds?", *Insight Turkey*, vol. 13, no. 1, winter 2011. Wexler is a former Member of Congress.

[76] Field and Zahedi, op. cit.

[77] See, e.g., Ariel Cohen, "Washington Concerned as Turkey Leaving the West," *Turkish Policy Quarterly*, vol. 9, no. 3, December 2010, available at http://www.turkishpolicy.com /dosyalar/files/25-35%281%29.pdf; Sally McNamara, Ariel Cohen, and James Phillips, "Countering Turkey's Strategic Drift," Heritage Foundation Backgrounder No. 2442, July 26, 2010, available at http://report.heritage.org/bg2442.

[78] See, e.g., Joshua Keating, "Turkey: Obama wanted us to make a deal with Iran," *foreignpolicy.com*, May 19, 2010.

[79] In the House, Representative Dina Titus sponsored H.Res. 1599, which was not passed but garnered 23 co-sponsors. H.Res. 1599 would have called upon the Secretary of State to investigate the "role of any foreign governments, including the Republic of Turkey, which may have aided and abetted the organizers of the recent Gaza Flotilla mission to breach Israeli coastal security and assault the naval defense forces of the State of Israel."

[80] James Traub, "Turkey's Rules," *New York Times Magazine*, January 20, 2011.

[81] For more information, see CRS Report R41549, *Missile Defense and NATO's Lisbon Summit*, by Steven A. Hildreth and Carl Ek.

[82] The joint explanatory statement is available at http://armed-services.senate.gov/Special %20Interest%20Item/ FINAL%20MASTER%20CONFERENCE%202010.pdf.

[83] Anders Fogh Rasmussen, "NATO Needs a Missile Defense," *New York Times*, October 12, 2010. However, in December 2010, a NATO-mandated industry advisory group reportedly concluded in an internal study that the cost could far exceed the early estimate. *Inside the Army* quoted the group's report as stating that "[w]hile NATO publicly envisages relatively benign cost for currently assumed territorial missile defence functionalities as add-on to the [existing theater-level missile defense] programme, it is obvious that a new, open [command-and-control] architecture approach will require a significant investment by NATO." "NATO Industry Report Says Missile Shield Cost Would Be 'Significant,'" *Inside the Army*, December 6, 2010.

[84] Kucukkosum, "Missile diplomacy latest test for US-NATO-Turk ties," op. cit.

[85] For a detailed discussion of AECA requirements respecting FMS and DCS, congressional options, and examples of congressional opposition to arms sales, see CRS Report RL31675, *Arms Sales: Congressional Review Process*, by Richard F. Grimmett. The congressional notice period is 30 days for FMS and DCS to non-NATO countries other than Japan, Australia, and New Zealand.

[86] "Procurement, Turkey," *Jane's Sentinel Security Assessment - Eastern Mediterranean*, December 16, 2010. Previous potential sales of Reapers to NATO allies such as the United Kingdom, Germany, and Italy were notified to Congress in 2008 and 2009 with the understanding that the drones would be used to support coalition operations in Iraq and Afghanistan.

[87] Ibid. Turkey may still operate two General Atomics GNATs (low altitude, low endurance reconnaissance drones) from a larger purchase it made from the United States in the 1990s.

[88] Ibid.

[89] For more information, see CRS Report RL30563, *F-35 Joint Strike Fighter (JSF) Program: Background and Issues for Congress*, by Jeremiah Gertler.

[90] Umit Enginsoy and Burak Ege Bekdil, "Turkey May Buy Up to 116 F-35s: Defense Minister," *Defense News*, January 24, 2011.

[91] "Procurement, Turkey," op. cit.

[92] Umit Enginsoy and Burak Ege Bekdil, "Turkey: We'll Make Our Own Fighter Jet," *Defense News*, December 20, 2010.

[93] Ercan Yavuz, "Problems persist with the US on fighter planes," *Today's Zaman*, January 23, 2011.

[94] Ercan Yavuz, "Defense giants compete in Turkish tender for long-range missiles," *Today's Zaman*, January 2, 2011. According to this report, the tender would be for four missile defense batteries, with possibly two more to be jointly produced with Turkish partners. At least one battery would be stationed in Istanbul and one in Ankara. Ibid.

[95] As mentioned earlier in the report, this committee is made up of the Prime Minister, the Chief of the General Staff, the Minister of National Defense, and the head of the separate procurement agency known as the Undersecretariat for Defense Industries (SSM).

[96] Yavuz, "Defense giants compete in Turkish tender for long-range missiles," op. cit.

[97] Ibid. According to the article, Russia would reportedly offer its family of S-400 systems.

[98] "An Assessment on the Developments Affecting the Current State and Shaping the Future of Turkish Naval Forces," *Defence Turkey*, vol. 5, no. 24, 2010.

[99] Chris Zambelis, "Sino-Turkish Partnership: Implications of Anatolian Eagle 2010," *China Brief*, vol. 11, no. 1, January 2011, available at http://www.jamestown.org /single /?no_cache=1&tx_ttnews[tt_news]=37369&tx_ttnews[backPid]=228&cHash=4b798b3435.

[100] Turkey and Russia entered into a number of defense cooperation agreements in 2005, including one focused on the Black Sea Naval Cooperation Task Group (BLACKSEAFOR) that involves all littoral Black Sea states (in addition to Turkey and Russia, this group includes Romania, Bulgaria, Georgia, and Ukraine). Russia, Turkey, and the other littoral states routinely participate in BLACKSEAFOR and Operation Black Sea Harmony exercises. "Armed forces, Turkey," op. cit. Turkey permits third-party-country naval access to the Black Sea through the Bosporus and Dardanelles Straits pursuant to the terms of the 1936 Montreux Convention, which can sometimes limit the size and volume of U.S. ships permitted to traverse the straits, as during the 2008 Russia-Georgia conflict.

[101] After Turkey signed a defense cooperation agreement with its former adversary Syria in 2002, the two countries held joint exercises in 2009 and 2010. Turkey's military also maintains close contacts and conducts joint exercises with Pakistan, as well as with smaller regional countries, such as Jordan, Kuwait, and the United Arab Emirates (UAE).

[102] Zambelis, op. cit.

[103] Kardas, "Davutoglu Outlines the Contours of the New Turkish Foreign Policy," op. cit.

[104] See, e.g., Guney, op. cit.

[105] Edward J. Erickson, "Turkey as Regional Hegemon—2014: Strategic Implications for the United States," *Turkish Studies*, vol. 5, no. 3, autumn 2004. Erickson is a retired Army Lieutenant Colonel who spent time stationed in Turkey and is now a professor at the U.S. Marine Corps University.

[106] The text of the CFE treaty is available at http://www.osce.org/library/14087. The text of an "Adapted CFE Treaty" that was signed by the parties to the original treaty (and, in some cases, their successors) at a 1999 Organization for Security and Cooperation in Europe (OSCE) summit but has not been ratified, along with the "Istanbul commitments" made by Russia and various other parties at the summit, is available at http://www.osce.org /mc/39569. Statements by Russia and NATO's North Atlantic Council relating to Russia's 2007 unilateral suspension of compliance with the treaty are available, respectively, at http://archive.kremlin.ru/eng/text/docs/2007/07/137839.shtml and http://www.nato.int/cps /en /SID-C29803BD-11807257/natolive/official_texts_8439.htm.

[107] Michael Robert Hickok, "Hegemon Rising: The Gap Between Turkish Strategy and Military Modernization," *Parameters*, vol. 30, no. 2, Summer 2000. Hickok wrote that according to Torumtay's memoirs, he and other senior officers disagreed with the decision because they felt that Turkey "lacked the indigenous military capability to sustain an independent foreign policy that risked a prolonged confrontation with its neighbors." Ibid.

[108] Cameron S. Brown, "Turkey in the Gulf Wars of 1991 and 2003," *Turkish Studies*, vol. 8, no. 1, March 2007.

[109] Ibid.

[110] Ibid.

[111] Ibid.

[112] Umit Enginsoy, "Turkish defense exports to Mideast unaffected by revolts," *Hurriyet Daily News & Economic Review*, March 6, 2011.

[113] The primary source for all of the examples is "Procurement - Turkey," op. cit.

[114] For an analysis of this procurement case and of Turkey's sometimes-criticized attempts to combine foreign procurement efforts—in this case involving the United States, Italy, and Russia—with greater indigenization of production, see Saban Kardas, "Turkey Considers Procuring Russian or American Attack Helicopters," *Eurasia Daily Monitor*, vol. 6, no. 116, June 17, 2009, available at http://www.jamestown.org/single/?no_cache=1& tx_ttnews[tt_news]=35139.

[115] Jorge Benitez, "7 NATO members sign agreement for military transport aircraft," *acus.org/natosource,* April 7, 2011.

[116] Enginsoy, "Turkish defense exports to Mideast unaffected by revolts," op. cit.

[117] Burak Ege Bekdil and Umit Enginsoy, "Turkey's 1st MALE UAV Makes Test Flight," *Defense News*, January 3, 2011.

[118] "Turkey - Defence Industry," *Jane's World Defence Industry*, July 21, 2010. Other export destinations include Malaysia, Saudi Arabia, Egypt, Syria, and Qatar. Enginsoy, "Turkish defense exports to Mideast unaffected by revolts," op. cit.

In: Turkey and the U.S.
Editors: S. N. Boothe and R. Hickman
ISBN: 978-1- 62081-276-1

Chapter 3

ISRAEL'S BLOCKADE OF GAZA, THE *MAVI MARMARA* INCIDENT, AND ITS AFTERMATH[†*]

Carol Migdalovitz

SUMMARY

Israel unilaterally withdrew from the Gaza Strip in 2005, but retained control of its borders. Hamas, a U.S. State Department-designated Foreign Terrorist Organization (FTO), won the 2006 Palestinian legislative elections and forcibly seized control of the territory in 2007. Israel imposed a tighter blockade of Gaza in response to Hamas's takeover and tightened the flow of goods and materials into Gaza after its military offensive against Hamas from December 2008 to January 2009. That offensive destroyed much of Gaza's infrastructure, but Israel has obstructed the delivery of rebuilding materials that it said could also be used to manufacture weapons and for other military purposes. Israel, the U.N., and international non-governmental organizations differ about the severity of the blockade's effects on the humanitarian situation of Palestinian residents of Gaza. Nonetheless, it is clear that the territory's economy and people are suffering.

---

† This is an edited, reformatted and augmented version of a Congressional Research Services publication, dated June 23, 2010.

* A version of this chapter also appears in *Hamas in the Middle East: A Closer Look*, edited by S. J. Wilkes and C. N. Jackson, published by Nova Science Publishers, Inc. It was submitted for appropriate modifications in an effort to encourage wider dissemination of research.

In recent years, humanitarian aid groups have sent supply ships and activists to Gaza. However, Israel directs them to its port of Ashdod for inspection before delivery to Gaza. In May 2010, the pro-Palestinian Free Gaza Movement and the pro-Hamas Turkish Humanitarian Relief Fund organized a six-ship flotilla to deliver humanitarian aid to Gaza and to break Israel's blockade of the territory. The ships refused an Israeli offer to deliver the goods to Ashdod. On May 31, Israeli naval special forces intercepted the convoy in international waters. They took control of five of the ships without resistance. However, some activists on a large Turkish passenger vessel challenged the commandos. The confrontation resulted in eight Turks and one Turkish-American killed, more than 20 passengers injured, and 10 commandos injured.

Israel considered its actions to be legitimate self-defense. Turkey, whose nationals comprised the largest contingent in the flotilla and among the casualties, considered them to be unjustifiable and in contravention of international law. There was near-universal international condemnation of Israel's actions. The U.N. Security Council in a U.S.-Turkish compromise condemned "the acts" that resulted in lost lives and called for an impartial inquiry. Several inquiries are underway in Israel, but Turkey will not be satisfied unless there is an international one under U.N. auspices.

The Obama Administration tried to walk a fine line between two allies, Israel and Turkey, and not allow the incident to derail efforts to ameliorate relations with Israel in order to protect Israeli-Palestinian talks now underway. It urged Israel to include international participants in its probe of the incident, and announced an aid package for the Palestinians that does not require new appropriations. However, the Administration's reaction displeased Turkey, and may contribute to that country's ongoing pursuit of a more independent foreign policy course. Turkish-Israeli relations, which had been deteriorating for some time, have reached a low point. In the aftermath of the incident, Israel has eased restrictions on the passage of goods and people into Gaza, while continuing to prevent shipments of weapons and dual-use items to Hamas.

BACKGROUND ON THE BLOCKADE

Israel withdrew from the Gaza Strip in 2005, but retained control of the territory's borders. Hamas emerged as the predominant force in the territory. In January 2006, Hamas won the Palestinian Authority (PA) legislative elections and established itself as a major actor in domestic politics. Some countries and organizations, including Turkey, consider Hamas a democratically elected, legitimate representative of the Palestinian people. Israel considers Hamas to be a terrorist group, and the U.S. State Department designates it as a Foreign Terrorist Organization (FTO). Hamas has criticized peace talks with Israel in line with its commitment to resistance, has perpetrated terrorist attacks against Israel, and has launched rockets from Gaza into Israel.

Hamas's participation in politics heightened its rivalry with Fatah, which had led all previous Palestinian governments.[1] It also prompted the United States to end all direct foreign aid to the Palestinians. Under pressure from Saudi Arabia, Hamas and Fatah formed a unity government in February 2007, which proved to be short-lived. In what it considered a pre-emptive act to prevent Fatah from striking it first, Hamas took control of the Gaza Strip by force in June 2007. This "coup" prompted PA President Mahmud Abbas to dissolve the Hamas-led government and replace it with the current one under Prime Minister Salam Fayyad, who administers only the West Bank. Hamas remains in control of Gaza. Israel and the United States reestablished relations with the new PA government, and Israel imposed a tight land, sea, and air blockade on the Gaza Strip, in what it describes as an act of self-defense to prevent arms from reaching Hamas. With the blockade, Israel also hoped to turn Gazans against Hamas by contrasting Hamas rule with the better life of Palestinians in the West Bank. Instead, the blockade isolated the territory and helped to strengthen Hamas's control.

From December 2008 to January 2009, Israeli forces carried out a major military offensive, called Operation Cast Lead, against Hamas in order to stop rocket fire into southern Israel and to weaken or overthrow Hamas. The campaign resulted in more than 1,000 Palestinian deaths and the destruction of much of the Gaza Strip's infrastructure and many buildings. Afterwards, Israel tightened the blockade and conditioned its end on the release of Israeli Defense Forces (IDF) Sergeant Gilad Shalit, who had been captured in 2006.

The blockade has severely affected the humanitarian situation in the Gaza Strip, although Israel and its critics differ about the effects. The Israeli government maintains that there is no humanitarian crisis in Gaza, and the IDF issues a detailed *Weekly Summary of Humanitarian Aid Transferred into Gaza* to support that position. The Ministry of Defense Coordinator of Government Activities in the Territories (COGAT) issues a similar *Gaza Strip Merchandise and Humanitarian Aid Report.* They provide information on the number of trucks and persons allowed to enter Gaza and list the cargos of food, medicine, and other supplies. The United Nations Office for the Coordination of Humanitarian Aid (OCHA) issues contrasting regular reports on the situation in Gaza. It summarily states that the blockade has "worsened conditions of life of

Palestinians, deepened poverty and food insecurity, prevented reconstruction, and increased aid dependence by destroying livelihoods and economic activity." It refers to the blockade as "collective punishment."[2] U.S. non-governmental humanitarian aid organizations, such as CARE and Mercy Corps, report difficulties experienced in rebuilding Gaza more than a year after Cast Lead, as well as obstacles that their workers face in trying to provide assistance because they cannot simultaneously accommodate U.S., Israeli, and Hamas rules—and Hamas is in control. Gazans have been unable to repair public infrastructure—hospitals, schools, electric systems, or sewage treatment plants—because Israel will not permit the delivery of materials such as steel, concrete, and tiles that could be used both for rebuilding and for the manufacture of weapons or other military purposes.[3]

In recent years, humanitarian aid groups have sent supply ships and activists to Gaza. However, Israel directs them to land at its port of Ashdod for inspection before delivery to Gaza. In addition to the deliveries allowed by Israel, Egypt intermittently opens the border crossing at Rafah with Gaza that it sealed in 2007.[4] Moreover, the smuggling of goods (and weapons) via a network of tunnels under the border also relieves the blockade somewhat, but smuggled goods create economic distortions by fueling a large informal economy. Israeli planes often bomb the tunnels, but these attacks have not put a stop to the activity.

RAID ON THE *MV MARMARA*

On May 22, 2010, the *MV Mavi Marmara*, a former Istanbul passenger ferry owned by the Turkish Humanitarian Relief Foundation (more fully the Foundation for Human Rights and Freedoms and Humanitarian Relief (IHH)), left Istanbul and, after stopping in the Mediterranean port of Antalya to pick up more than 500 passengers, met up at sea with five other ships south of Cyprus. IHH also sent two cargo vessels. Several ships from the Free Gaza Movement had departed from the Greek port of Piraeus. A six-ship flotilla then set sail for the Gaza Strip with the intent to deliver 10,000 tons of humanitarian aid and to break the Israeli blockade. In all, about 700 activists from 38 countries participated in the expedition, including approximately 11 Americans, some European parliamentarians, and Swedish writer Henning Mankell. On May 30, the ships refused Israel's offer to unload at the port of Ashdod so that their cargos could be inspected before delivery accompanied by representatives of the non-governmental organizations.

On May 31, when the ships were in international waters between 80 and 100 miles from the Israeli coast, Israeli navy zodiac boats intercepted them and naval commandos took over five ships, reportedly without incident. However, the *Marmara* resisted and commandos rappelled from helicopters onto that ship and were confronted by some passengers/activists. The IDF released videos showing that individuals attacking the commandos were armed with iron rods, knives, broken glass bottles, and sling shots, and equipped with gas masks, night vision goggles, and life vests. The IDF says that the passengers also seized a commando's side arm. IHH President Bulent Yildirim admitted that activists had used iron rods, but claimed that they threw seized Israeli weapons into the sea.[5] It is not clear if the commandos, who had paintball guns and firearms, struck first or in response to an attack from the passengers, and each side has given a different account. Nine passengers were killed, including eight Turks and a Turkish-American; 24 were injured, including one American, and 10 commandos were injured. The dead were members of or volunteers for IHH, which hailed them as "martyrs."

All of the ships were taken to Ashdod, where the passengers were detained and the cargo was unloaded, inspected, and trucked to the Kerem Shalom border crossing between Israel and Gaza. Hamas initially refused to allow the aid to be transferred into Gaza and the Israeli Defense Ministry stored it at a military base while it consulted international organizations. On June 15, it was announced that the U.N. would distribute the aid. By June 3, Israel had deported all the detainees, including all alleged perpetrators of the attacks on its military personnel, except for a few severely wounded who were repatriated a few days later.

Israeli officials claim to have found Molotov cocktails, detonators, wood and metal clubs, slingshots and rocks, large hammers, and sharp metal objects on the *Marmara*, but no rockets.[6]

IHH and the Free Gaza Movement

The flotilla was the idea of the Free Gaza Movement, which teamed up with the IHH. The Free Gaza Movement is a Cyprus-based coalition or alliance formed to oppose Israel's blockade of the Gaza Strip and is said to have roots in the International Solidarity Movement, a non-violent movement dedicated to ending the Israeli occupation of Palestinian territory.[7] Its members had sailed to Gaza several times before, and Israel had let them dock there five times. After Operation Cast Lead, however, Israel began intercepting Free Gaza Movement ships before they reached Gaza. This year, Free Gaza decided to cooperate with other groups, including the IHH, in a "freedom" flotilla.[8] Free Gaza Movement founder Greta Berlin said that former Malaysian Prime Minister Mahathir Mohammed had raised €300,000 (approximately $367,000) to enable the Movement's participation in the convoy.[9] She said that it will continue to send ships to Gaza, and Israel peacefully intercepted another one, the *MV Rachel Corrie*, on June 5.

IHH is a humanitarian aid organization founded in 1995 that is said to have ties to the International Red Cross; holds special consultative status with the U.N. Economic, Social, and Cultural Organization (UNESCO); and operates in more than 100 countries.[10] It has provided humanitarian aid to Bosnia and Chechnya as well as to victims of Hurricane Katrina and the earthquake in Haiti, among other activities. IHH's involvement with the aid flotilla is in line with its previous aid to Gaza, where it has an office. In addition to the *Mavi Marmara*, IHH contributed two cargo ships to the May convoy.

Days before the raid, an Israeli think tank released a report linking IHH to radical Islamist networks, including Hamas and the Muslim Brotherhood, and to "global jihad elements" in the 1990s. It cited a French intelligence report claim that IHH President Bulent Yildirim had recruited Muslims for jihad in Bosnia, Chechnya, and Afghanistan in the 1990s, but also stated that IHH engages in "legitimate humanitarian activities."[11] Since the incident, the think tank has released additional reports, including one alleging that IHH employed violence on the *Mavi Marmara* with premeditation.[12]

IHH openly supports Hamas, which led Israel to outlaw it in 2008. It is not a U.S. State Department-designated terrorist group, although it is part of a Saudi-based, Hamas-created umbrella group of Muslim charities called Union of Good that the U.S. Treasury has designated as a terrorist organization.[13]

IHH has influential connections in Turkey. In his remarks at the *Marmara*'s departure from Istanbul, Yildirim thanked the ruling Justice and Development Party (AKP) and two small Islamist parties for their support. IHH is believed to be close to the conservative Islamist Felicity Party (SP). While there was no direct Turkish government involvement in the aid mission, government administrators facilitated IHH's purchase of the ferry from the Istanbul municipality, which AKP controls, and its departure from Turkish ports. Yildirim also mentioned recent instances of IHH aid workers' "martyrdom" in Afghanistan and imprisonment in Israel, and IHH leaders have referred to those killed on the *Marmara* as "martyrs."[14] IHH is said to have had about 40 to 50 members aboard the *Marmara*.

VIEWS FROM ISRAEL

While there is a multiplicity of views in Israel concerning the blockade of Gaza and the raid on the *Marmara*, most Israelis equate security with survival and peace. Israel's leaders appear to believe that the blockade of the Gaza Strip, the security barrier that Israel has constructed in the West Bank, the successes of the Palestinian security forces and economy in the West Bank, and what it views as enhanced deterrence in the aftermath of military campaigns against Hezbollah in Lebanon in 2006 and Hamas in the Gaza Strip from December 2008 to January 2009 have brought about a kind of quiet, if not peace. As of the date of the incident, no Israeli had been killed in a terrorist attack or a cross-border rocket attack in Israel in more than a year. Therefore, the government is unwilling to abandon a tactic (i.e., the blockade) that has worked—and is still working from its perspective. Prime Minister Benjamin Netanyahu insists that the blockade is necessary to prevent weapons from reaching Gaza. He maintains, "(I)t's our obligation—as well as our right in accordance to international law and to common sense—to prevent these weapons from entering by air, sea, and land."[15] He cites two earlier examples of Israel's seizure of ships that were discovered to be carrying arms.

The prime minister claimed that the flotilla intercepted in May intended to break the naval blockade, not to bring goods, and said Israel allows goods and cargo to enter Gaza. He added, "Had the blockade been breached, this flotilla would have been followed by dozens, by hundreds of ships. The amount of weapons that can be transported aboard a ship is totally different from what we saw get through the tunnels (beneath the Gaza-Egypt border). Hundreds of missiles and rockets, and an innumerable number of weapons can be smuggled aboard a ship."[16]

Netanyahu argued that the consequences of Israel's failure to maintain the blockade would be "an Iranian port in Gaza, only a few dozen kilometers from Tel Aviv and Jerusalem." Israeli officials refer to those killed on the *Marmara* as "terrorists" and, as noted above, Israel banned the IHH in 2008.

VIEWS FROM TURKEY

As noted, several Turkish political parties, including the ruling AKP, supported the IHH effort to aid the Palestinians. However, the Turkish government claims it was not directly involved. Foreign Minister Ahmet

Davutoglu said afterwards that the government had tried to convince the non-governmental organizations in charge of the flotilla to take the aid to Israeli ports, but it was not successful.[17] The government also urged Israel to let the ships land in Gaza.

The Turkish government, all political parties, and people were outraged by the Israeli attack. After the raid, mass demonstrations occurred in Ankara and Istanbul, and officials made repeated, dramatic, if not hyperbolic, statements about Israel's actions. The Turkish Foreign Ministry first protested Israel's use of force "in the strongest terms," charging that "Israel has once again clearly demonstrated that it does not value human lives and peaceful initiatives through targeting innocent civilians."[18]

Turkey called for an emergency meeting of the U.N. Security Council—on which it holds a nonpermanent seat—that Foreign Minister Davutoglu attended on May 31. Turkey also called for NATO permanent representatives in Brussels and the Organization of the Islamic Conference (OIC), which it chairs, to meet on the issue. At the Security Council session, Davutoglu called Israel's actions "banditry and piracy ... murder conducted by a state ... and barbarism." He stated that the use of force was "inappropriate" and "disproportionate" and that international law dictates that "even in wartime, civilians are not to be attacked or harmed." He argued that the doctrine of self-defense could not justify the actions of Israeli forces.[19] Finally, he called on the council to condemn Israel's "act of aggression," demand an urgent inquiry, and call for the punishment of all responsible authorities and persons.

Prime Minister Recep Tayyip Erdogan described Israel's actions as a "bloody massacre" deserving "every kind of curse." He said, "This insolent, irresponsible, reckless, and unfair attack by the Israeli government which trampled on every kind of human value must be punished by all means."[20] These quotes are characteristic of his many unsparing, trenchant remarks. The most offensive and inflammatory may have been his blaming Israel for increasingly common global comparisons of the "Zionist star" (i.e., Star of David) with the Nazi swastika.[21]

For some time, Turkish officials' anti-Israeli rhetoric have gained them considerable regional influence. Erdogan is very popular with Arab publics and his fervor and rage also benefit him with voters. While the heat of the first days after the raid may dissipate, the anger will remain. The prime minister may be feeding or exploiting it for domestic political purposes in the run-up to national elections next year, or earlier, as he cannot afford to lose votes to either more Islamist parties or the reviving secular opposition.

INTERNATIONAL REACTIONS

There has been near-universal condemnation of Israel's actions. Nicaragua broke off relations with Israel, while Ecuador and South Africa recalled their ambassadors and many other governments called in Israeli ambassadors to protest. The European Union reiterated its demand for an immediate opening of Gaza's border crossings. China urged Israel to end the blockade and condemned the Israeli raid on the ship. Russia called on Israel to lift the blockade and for an impartial investigation.

U.N. Secretary General Ban Ki-moon condemned the violence and called for a full investigation. The U.N. Human Rights Council voted to launch an independent, international inquiry into the events, although the United States voted against it. On June 1, a compromise Statement by the President of the Security Council at the U.N. regretted "the loss of life and injuries resulting from the use of force during the Israeli military operation in international waters against the convoy sailing to Gaza.... The Council ... condemns those acts which resulted in the loss of at least ten civilians and many wounded." It called for a "prompt, impartial, credible, and transparent investigation conforming to international standards." In addition, the council reiterated its "grave concern at the humanitarian situation in Gaza" and stressed "the need for sustained regular flow of goods and people to Gaza as well as unimpeded provision and distribution of humanitarian assistance throughout Gaza." It again called for a two-state solution to the Israeli-Palestinian conflict and expressed support for the ongoing proximity talks (that are being mediated by U.S. Special Envoy for Middle East Peace George Mitchell).[22]

British Prime Minister David Cameron called Israel's actions "unacceptable." He said that Britain remained committed to Israel's security and urged Netanyahu to respond constructively to "legitimate" international criticism and to lift the blockade.[23] German Chancellor Angela Merkel expressed her "deep concern" to both Netanyahu and Erdogan, and her spokesman said, "Every German government has always recognized and supported the right of Israel to defend itself, but this right must of course be within the bounds of proportionality."[24] French President Nicolas Sarkozy condemned "the disproportionate use of force" and said, "All possible light must be shed on the circumstances surrounding this tragedy, which highlights the urgent need for the peace process to be relaunched."[25]

On June 14, the Council of the European Union adopted conclusions regretting the loss of life during Israel's military operation in international waters against the flotilla sailing to Gaza and condemned the use of violence.

It called of an immediate, full, and impartial inquiry with credible international participation. It called for "the immediate, sustained, and unconditional opening of crossings for the flow of humanitarian aid, commercial goods, and person to and from Gaza" and "for a solution that addresses Israel's legitimate security concerns."[26]

INVESTIGATIONS/INQUIRIES

In response to international calls for an investigation of the incident, Israel has launched several probes. On June 7, Israel Defense Forces (IDF) Chief of Staff Lt. Gen. Gabi Ashkenazi appointed former head of the National Security Council Maj. Gen. Giora Eiland (Ret.) to head an external military probe that will report by July 4. Three other retired senior officers are on the panel that is tasked with drawing operational conclusions. It reportedly will delve into the choice of unit to carry out the operation, possible alternative tactics that might have been used to stop the flotilla, military decision-making leading up to the operation, and intelligence matters.[27] Eiland has already defended the commandos' right to self-defense and said, "(T)here was a mistake, but not on the soldiers' part. The mistake lay in underestimating who the Turkish ship's passengers were."[28]

On June 13, Prime Minister Netanyahu announced the establishment of a special, independent public commission to inquire into the events of May 31. It will be chaired by retired Supreme Court Justice Jacob Turkel, who still sits on a military appeals court panel, and, as members, Shabtai Rosen, a professor of international law and former diplomat, and Maj. Gen. Amos Horen (Ret.), a former president of Technion (Israel Institute of Technology). The panel includes two foreign observers: Lord David Trimble, the former first minister of Northern Ireland, and Brig. Gen. Ken Watkin, former judge advocate general of the Canadian Forces.

The commission has a limited mandate. It will investigate whether Israel's blockade of the Gaza Strip and the enforcement of it conform to international law. It also will consider the actions and identities of those who organized and participated in the flotilla. Military personnel will not be required to testify. Instead, the IDF will provide it with summaries of the Eiland investigation.[29]

Israel had coordinated its approach to the investigation with the Obama Administration, which had urged the inclusion of an "international component" to enhance the inquiry's credibility. Hence, the White House reaction to the Israeli announcement was positive:

> We believe that Israel, like any other nation, should be allowed to undertake an investigation into events that involve its national security. Israel has a military justice system that meets international standards and is capable of conducting a serious and credible investigation, and the structure and terms of reference of Israel's proposed independent public commission can meet the standard of a prompt, impartial, credible, and transparent investigation. But we will not prejudge the process or its outcome, and will await the conduct and findings of the investigation before drawing further conclusions.[30]

However, Turkish Foreign Minister Davutoglu was not satisfied. He declared,

> The crime was committed in international waters, not in Israel's territorial waters. A commission which will conduct an inquiry into an attack staged in international waters should be international. We demand that an international commission should be formed under the supervision of the U.N. with participation of Turkey and Israel.... We believe that Israel, as a country which attacked on a civil convoy in international waters, will not conduct an impartial inquiry.[31]

He also said that "international participation in a commission established by Israel does not give it an international quality."[32] Finally, Davutoglu stated that if an international commission were not set up, then Turkey would unilaterally review its ties with Israel and implement sanctions against it.

Israel's State Comptroller Micha Lindenstrauss will carry out yet another investigation into the legality of the government's decision-making as well as intelligence and public relations issues. The probe will not duplicate that of the IDF or the Turkel group.

Meanwhile, U.N. Secretary General Ban Ki-moon took note of the Israeli announcement, but added that his own proposal for an international inquiry remains on the table and he hoped for a positive Israeli response. Turkey accepted Ban's proposal and called on Israel to do so. However, Israeli Defense Minister Ehud Barak said, after meeting the Secretary General and providing details concerning new steps to ease the blockade (see "The Blockade," below) "we consider an [international probe] while organizations that support terror are trying to send more ships to Gaza to be an irresponsible act."[33]

On June 17, the Turkish Foreign Ministry announced that a panel headed by the foreign and justice ministers "will assess the national and international dimensions" of the raid and prepare the ground for a possible international investigation.[34]

U.S. Position

Policy

The United States is caught between two long-time allies—Israel and Turkey—and the Obama Administration seems interested in finding a path between them that will not antagonize either party. It is a challenging task. State Department spokesman P.J. Crowley reported that, before the raid, the Administration had urged caution and restraint on Israel given the anticipated presence of civilians, including American civilians.[35]

Afterwards, the Administration's first reaction was circumspect, if not muted. The White House issued a statement saying, "The President expressed deep regret at the loss of life in today's incident and concern for the wounded.... The President also expressed the importance of learning all the facts and circumstances surrounding this morning's tragic events as soon as possible."[36]

The Administration negotiated with Turkey concerning the Security Council President's statement that condemned "acts" resulting in the loss of life, but not Israel per se. The statement also did not call for an international investigation because of recent experience with what Israel and the Administration considered to be the one-sided U.N. Goldstone Commission investigation of Operation Cast Lead. The State Department's Crowley indicated that the United States believes "Israel is in the best position to conduct an investigation."[37] U.S. Deputy Permanent Representative at the U.N. Alejandro D. Wolff also criticized the attempt to break the blockade, saying, "Direct delivery by sea is neither appropriate nor responsible, and certainly not effective, under the circumstances." Yet, he further said that the situation in Gaza was "unsustainable."[38] Secretary of State Hillary Rodham Clinton made the same observation.

The White House said that President Obama "affirmed the importance of finding better ways to provide humanitarian assistance to the people of Gaza without undermining Israel's security."[39] Vice President Biden maintained that because Israel is at war with Hamas, it "has a right to know whether or not arms are being smuggled in."[40] He also stated that the Administration had been "cajoling" Israel to allow building materials into Gaza.

The Administration likely does not want its reaction to the flotilla incident to further disrupt what has become an uneasy bilateral relationship with Israel. It needs a better relationship with the Netanyahu government in order to make progress in the Israeli-Palestinian peace talks, which U.S. officials believe to be in America's national security interests. Strains had developed due to President Obama's and Netanyahu's differing views regarding West Bank settlement activity and, especially, Jerusalem. The Administration does not want Israel to take any actions that could prejudge a final settlement with the Palestinians, who seek a state in the West Bank and Gaza with east Jerusalem as its capital. The incident at sea led Prime Minister Netanyahu to cancel a June 1 meeting with President Obama at the White House, but it has been rescheduled for July 6.

At the same time, the Administration needed to consider the strength of its desire for Turkey's support in the Security Council for sanctions on Iran. It is usually believed that unanimity or a large number of votes in the council lends greater weight on such issues. It is possible, however, that the Administration had decided to proceed without Turkey's support, given the announcement in Tehran on May 17 of an agreement with Iran and Brazil on an exchange in Turkey of some of Iran's low enriched uranium for medical grade uranium—a deal that the Administration found deficient. Turkey voted against sanctions, which its officials maintain was because of the Tehran deal and not related to the events of May 31 and their aftermath.

Aid

On June 9, at a meeting with Palestinian Authority (PA) President Abbas, President Obama promised $400 million in aid for the West Bank and Gaza Strip. None of the aid requires new congressional action as all was appropriated in FY2009 and FY2010 legislation. Most is not for Gaza.[41] That slated in some way for Gaza includes $40 million to support the United Nations Relief and Works Agency's (UNRWA) Emergency Appeal for Gaza and the West Bank to help improve educational and health services, increase job creation, and repair shelters in Gaza, while also addressing core humanitarian needs in the West Bank; $14.5 million for school rehabilitation, small-scale agriculture, the repair of a hospital and other community infrastructure in Gaza; $10 million for the construction of five new UNRWA schools in Gaza; and $5 million to complete five USAID-funded projects to repair water distribution and wastewater collection systems in Gaza.

IMPLICATIONS FOR THE FUTURE

The Blockade

There is an international consensus that something must be done to lift or ease Israel's blockade of Gaza and to reestablish a fully functioning economy there for its residents. Yet, there was a dearth of ideas from those who called on Israel to end the blockade concerning creative ways for Israel to do that and to continue to prevent the arming of Hamas and its development as a more deadly threat to Israel. Hamas is exploiting the flotilla incident as a propaganda victory. It is not in the group's interest to not attempt to rearm or to help lessen Israel's international isolation. It is in the United States' and international community's interest to find a solution to this problem.

President Obama described the situation in Gaza as "unsustainable." He stated "we agree that Israelis have the right to prevent arms from entering into Gaza that can be used to launch attacks into Israeli territory. But ... it is important for us to explore new mechanisms so that we can have goods and services, and economic development, and the ability of people to start their own businesses, and to grow the economy and provide opportunity within Gaza." He added, "there should be ways of focusing narrowly on arms shipments, rather than focusing in a blanket way on stopping everything and then in a piecemeal way allowing things into Gaza."[42]

The Israeli government discussed ways to ease procedures at land crossings. Prime Minister Netanyahu insisted that the sea blockade is essential. Foreign Minister Avigdor Lieberman suggested that Israel offer to ease the crossings in exchange for monthly International Red Cross visits to Sergeant Gilad Shalit. However, Hamas restated its position that any movement on Shalit depends solely on Israel's release of more than 1,000 Palestinian prisoners, as it has long demanded, and is not related to any other issue.[43]

One suggestion was for Israel to publish a limited list of goods prohibited for security reasons and let all other goods enter the Gaza Strip. Former British Prime Minister Tony Blair, the Quartet Representative, and the European Union urged Israel to adopt the practice and it did "in principle." On June 17, Prime Minister Netanyahu's office announced that the Israeli security cabinet had agreed to "liberalize the system by which civilian goods enter Gaza; expand the inflow of materials for civilian projects that are under international supervision; continue existing security procedures to prevent the inflow of weapons and war materiel; and to decide in the coming days on additional steps to implement this policy."[44] However, the naval blockade would not be lifted. The White House welcomed the move as "a step in the right direction. On June 20, the Prime Minister's Office announced the following steps to be implemented "as quickly as possible":

- Publish a list of items not permitted into Gaza that is limited to weapons and war materiel, including problematic dual-use items. All items not on the list will be permitted.
- Enable and expand the inflow of dual-use construction materials for Palestinian Authority-approved projects (schools, health facilities, water, sanitation, etc.) that are under international supervision and for U.N. housing projects.
- Expand operations at the existing operating land crossings, thereby enabling the processing of a significantly greater volume of goods and the expansion of economic activity.
- Add substantial capacity at the existing operating land crossings and, as necessary, add additional land crossings.
- Streamline the policy of permitting the entry and exit of people for humanitarian and medical reasons and that of employees of international aid organizations recognized by the government of Israel.
- Continue the inspection and delivery of goods bound for Gaza through the port of Ashdod.[45]

The White House responded, "Once implemented, we believe these arrangements should significantly improve conditions for Palestinians in Gaza, while preventing the entry of weapons." It also wanted to "explore additional ways to improve the situation in Gaza, including freedom of movement and commerce between Gaza and the West Bank."[46] The measures have not put an end to calls for a complete lifting of the blockade. The Turkish Foreign Ministry said that they were "a positive step but not enough."[47] Meanwhile, Sergeant Shalit's father charged that the Israeli government had surrendered an important tool to gain his son's release.

Shortly after the *Marmara* incident Egypt announced the opening of the Rafah crossing "indefinitely," although it only allowed travelers with special permits and continued to restrict potentially dual use goods.

Some PA officials are concerned that efforts to lift the blockade will lead to a more autonomous Gaza Strip that is permanently separate from the West Bank. Such concerns may have animated Prime Minister Fayyad's suggestion, also proposed by Tony Blair and others, to reinstate the 2005 Agreement on Movement and Access, which called, *inter alia*, for the Rafah border crossing to operate with EU monitors and Israeli surveillance as well as for a link between Gaza and the West Bank.[48] PA forces also were situated at the border. The EU Border Assistance Mission (EU-BAM) operated until suspended when Hamas took over the Gaza Strip in 2007. Its revival would be a way for the PA to reestablish its forces at the border. However, a Hamas spokesman quickly declared, "any international intervention, especially by the Europeans, must come through the government of Gaza," which would be problematic for both the PA and the Europeans.[49]

New attempts to break the blockade are expected. The Iranian Red Crescent announced plans to send three ships and one airplane bearing supplies for Gaza, but delivery may be made via the Egyptian Red Crescent. The European Campaign to End the Siege on Gaza says that it is organizing another aid flotilla. A ship with women activists carrying food and medicine already has set sail from Lebanon and others from Reporters without Borders and the Free Palestine Movement plan to leave from there as well. The IHH announced that it has assembled six ships for another flotilla due to sail in the second half if July that it invited others to join. The Israeli Foreign Ministry spokesman said that ships from Iran and Lebanon are from "enemy states" and would get different treatment.[50] The U.S. State Department has tried to discourage these efforts, stating, "everyone who wants to help the people of Gaza should work through established channels."

Israeli-Palestinian Peace Talks

Many observers believe that the best response to the current crisis and the way to prevent future ones is Israeli-Palestinian peace and the creation of an independent Palestinian state that would deprive Hamas of its resistance rationale and lead to better lives for the Palestinians. U.S. Special Envoy for Middle East Peace George Mitchell says that the proximity talks that have been underway for several weeks between Prime Minister Netanyahu and President Abbas will continue. Abbas also has stated that the talks will not be broken off. However, few are optimistic about the prospects for peace given the uncompromising territorial ambitions of right-wing nationalists in the Netanyahu government and the divided Palestinian rule between Gaza and the West Bank. Even if an accord can be achieved, many wonder how successfully it can be implemented.

Turkish-Israeli Relations

The current crisis is undoubtedly a turning point in Turkish-Israeli relations. President Abdullah Gul declared, "Turkish-Israeli relations can never be as before from now on."[51] Yet, this change is not dramatic; it has been coming for some time.

The picture of Turkish-Israeli friendship was drawn in the 1990s when their bilateral relations improved in tandem with Israeli-Palestinian peace talks and when both governments viewed Syria, then their common neighbor, as an adversary. Cordiality was aided by the Turkish military's appreciation of Israeli arms for use in the fight with Kurdistan Workers Party (PKK) insurgents. Joint military exercises became routine. Surprising to some, relations did not deteriorate when the Justice and Development Party (AKP), which has Islamist roots, came to power in 2002. Prime Minister Erdogan visited Israel and Israeli President Shimon Peres addressed the Turkish parliament. Israel trusted Ankara enough to allow it to mediate indirect peace talks with Syria in 2008.

However, Israel's suspicions of the AKP may have been sparked when the party hosted Hamas Politburo Chief Khalid Mish'al in 2006, after the Palestinian Authority legislative elections. Turkish officials repeatedly refer to Hamas as a democratically elected group that was denied the chance to govern, and call on the international community to engage Hamas. Moreover, Israel is aware of Turkey's close relations with Iran, its defense of that country's right to develop nuclear energy, and its charge that the international community uses a double standard when it fails to castigate Israel for its nuclear weapons. Erdogan and other Turkish officials almost always refer to Israel's nuclear weapons when countering international concern about the possibility that Iran seeks such weapons; Erdogan has described that notion as "gossip." Turkish officials do not, as Israeli officials do, refer to Iranian President Mahmud Ahmadinejad's vow to "wipe Israel off the map" or to Iran's support for anti-Israel terrorists. In other words, a gap has been widening between the two erstwhile friends.

Bilateral relations have been deteriorating rapidly since Israel's military campaign against Hamas from December 2008 to January 2009. Prime Minister Erdogan has said that he was insulted that then Israeli Prime Minister Ehud Olmert had failed to inform him of the anticipated offensive while in Turkey for consultations regarding the Turkish-mediated Israeli-Syrian peace talks just days before launching the offensive. In January 2009, Erdogan took offense at President Peres's defense of Operation Cast Lead at the World

Economic Forum and stormed off the stage. Erdogan's action gained him popularity throughout the Arab world. Shortly thereafter, a Turkish television series depicted Israeli soldiers as barbarians. Erdogan has repeatedly criticized Prime Minister Netanyahu's government. In October 2009, Turkey cancelled Israel's participation in a multilateral military exercise—some suggested that this was due to concerns that Israel would use it to prepare for an attack on Iran. In January 2010, Israeli Deputy Prime Minister Dani Ayalon insulted Turkey's ambassador to Israel while complaining about the television series. Turkey demanded and received an apology. Erdogan is unrelenting in his repeated references to what he refers to as Israel's inhumane conduct of the Gaza campaign and of its continuing ill treatment of the Palestinians in Gaza, which he calls an "open air prison." He also has warned Israel not to try to change the character of Jerusalem and questioned the Jews' ties to certain religious sites.

After Israel's raid on the flotilla, Erdogan said "Today is a turning point in history. Nothing will be the same again," speaking of relations with Israel.[52] Turkey recalled its ambassador from Israel and cancelled three joint military drills, cooperation in the fields of energy and water, and soccer matches. It also is demanding that Israel apologize and compensate the victims. Foreign Minister Davutoglu says that relations will not improve until the results of an international probe of the Israeli raid are implemented and Israel lifts the siege of Gaza.

Defense Minister Vecdi Gonul said that Turkey did not plan to cancel military contracts for the purchase of Israeli arms, including Heron drones, radars, and avionic systems, and joint production of mine-resistant ambush-protected (MRAP) vehicles.[53] Most of the Herons have been delivered and Israel has been compensated for them. However, after the flotilla incident, Israeli defense industries withdrew engineers and flight officers who were training Turkish forces for the Heron. The companies also claimed that the deal had not been cancelled and, on June 22, a Turkish military delegation arrived in Israel to test the last four drones scheduled for delivery. Much of the Turkish-Israeli bilateral trade—worth $2.5 billion in 2009—has been Turkey's purchase of military equipment from Israel and it was anticipated to increase before the incident. The two countries signed a free trade agreement in 1996. Observers do not believe that any new deals should be expected.

Aside from criticizing Israel's plans for its own inquiry into the incident, Foreign Minister Davutoglu declared that Turkey would work to isolate Israel in every international platform if an international investigation were not established.[54]

U.S.-Turkish Relations

The flotilla crisis may have added to a developing rift in the foreign policies of Turkey and the United States. The Administration does not want to harm relations with Turkey, which is important to U.S. geostrategic interests, particularly in Iraq and Afghanistan. President Obama called Prime Minister Erdogan to convey his condolences for the tragedy at sea. However, some in Turkey want the Administration to choose between Israel and Turkey, and believe that the United States must choose Turkey. As that is unlikely, some Turks may remain unsatisfied.

Despite its NATO membership and European Union candidacy, Turkey is an increasingly independent actor on the international stage, reflective of its growing economic and regional power and ambition to be a world power. It is conforming less automatically than in the past to the views of the United States and other Western allies, and developing what Foreign Minister Davutoglu has described as a "multidirectional" foreign policy. Ankara also is less reluctant to criticize its American ally publicly. With regard to the flotilla incident, Davutoglu expressed disappointment with Washington's "cautious reaction to the events."[55] He stated, "We expect full solidarity with us. It should not seem like a choice between Turkey and Israel. It should be a choice between right and wrong, between legal and illegal."[56] He also complained that the United States had delayed and watered down the U.N. Security Council President's statement.

This crisis came on the heels of a disagreement between Washington and Ankara over Turkey's agreement with Brazil and Iran concerning Iran's uranium. Davutoglu insists that Turkey followed guidance in an October 2009 letter from President Obama to Prime Minister Erdogan in formulating the deal, but the U.S. State Department had observed several weeks before the agreement was announced in Tehran that those parameters needed updating. The Foreign Minister also sought to place the agreement with Iran in the context of President Obama's policies of engagement and multilateralism in order to deprive United States of room to maneuver in its effort to get harsher sanctions imposed on Iran. As noted above, Turkey voted against sanctions.

Recent events suggest U.S. policy makers should expect additional and increasing examples of Turkey's developing autonomous foreign policy. It may be a challenge for U.S. officials to accommodate their views to Turkey's "multidirectionalism" or to address it constructively.

LEGISLATION

S.Res. 548, introduced and referred to the Committee on Foreign Relations on June 9, 2010. To express the sense of the Senate that Israel has an undeniable right to self-defense, and to condemn the recent destabilizing actions by extremists aboard the *Mavi Marmara*.

H.R. 5501, American Stands with Israel Act, introduced and referred to the Committee on Foreign Affairs on June 10, 2010. To prohibit the United States participation on the U.N. Human Rights Council and prohibit contributions to the U.N. for the purpose of paying for any U.N. investigation into the flotilla incident.

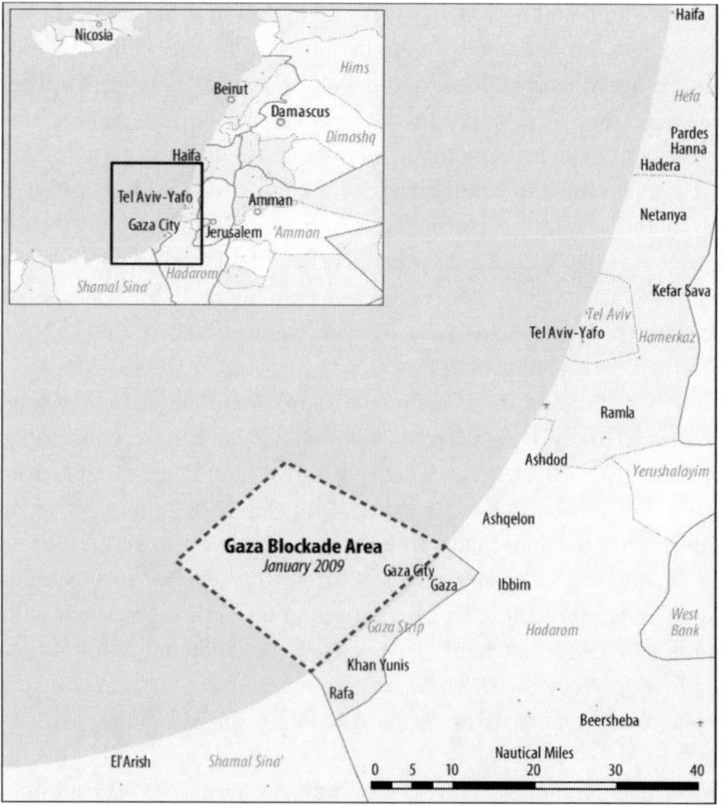

Source: Produced by CRS based on State of Israel, Ministry of Transport, Notice to Mariners, No. 1/2009 Blockade of Gaza Strip, January 2009; ESRI Community Data, 2008.

Figure 1. Blockade of Gaza.

End Notes

[1] For background on Palestinian politics, see CRS Report RL34074, *The Palestinians: Background and U.S. Relations*,
by Jim Zanotti.

[2] "Statement of John Holmes, USG for Humanitarian Affairs and Relief Coordinator on the 'Free Gaza' Flotilla Crisis," June 2, 2010, http://www.ochaopt.org. The Israeli non-governmental organization B'tselem (Israeli Information Center for Human Rights in the Occupied Territories) issued a report with similar findings. See http://www.bvtselem.org/English/Gaza_Strip/20100531/The_Siege_on_Gaza.asp.

[3] Janine Zacharia, "Getting What They Need to Live, but not Thrive," *Washington Post*, June 3, 2010.

[4] Egypt sealed the border out of concern for the possibly destabilizing effects of Hamas's relations with the Egyptian Muslim Brotherhood, which the government of President Mubarak considers a threat.

[5] "Humanitarian Foundation says People Still Missing from Aid Convoy," Anatolia, June 3, 2010, Open Source Center Document GMP20100603744008.

[6] "Israel's Vilna'i Implies Ships 'Sabotaged,' Army Video Shows Seized Weapons," OSC Summary, Open Source Center Document GMP201006-1739005.

[7] Sabrina Tavernise, Michael Slackman, "Turkish Funds Helped Group Test Blockade of Gaza," *New York Times*, June 1, 2010. The International Solidarity Movement (ISM) states that it is "a Palestinian-led movement committed to resisting the Israeli occupation of Palestinian land using non-violent, direct-action methods and principles." See http://www.palsolidarity.org.

[8] Sabrina Tavernise, Michael Slackman, "Turks' Gifts Gave Flotilla Activists New Life," *New York Times*, June 3, 2010.

[9] Marc Champion, Margaret Coker, "Confrontation at Sea: Turkish Charity Sounds a Defiant Note," *Wall Street Journal*, June 4, 2010.

[10] Marc Champion, "Confrontation at Sea: Turkish Aid Organization Draws Controversy," *Wall Street Journal*, June 2, 2010.

[11] "Israel Intel Center Profiles 'Islamic, Anti-Western' Turkish IHH Organization," report by Ramat Hasharon Intelligence and Terrorism Information Center (an NGO), May 26, 2010, Open Source Center Document GMP20100530739004. The French investigating judge who authored the report told the Associated Press that IHH had "clear, longstanding ties to terrorism and jihad" and that part of the NGO served to hide jihad-type activities in the late 1990s, Alfred De Montesquiou, "Investigator Says Flotilla's Donor Linked to Terror," *Boston Globe*, June 3, 2010.

[12] "Additional Information about the Violent Intentions of the IHH Operatives During the Voyage of the Mavi Marmara and the Weapons Found in their Possession," Intelligence and Terrorism Information Center, June 10, 2010, Open Source Center Document GMP20100615739012, June 15, 2010.

[13] See U.S. Treasury Designates the Union of Good, HP1267, November 12, 2008, http://www.ustreas.gov/press/ releases/hp1267.htm.

[14] "Turkey: 'Mavi Marmara Ship' Leaves Istanbul Harbor Towards Gaza to Deliver Aid," May 24, 2010, Open Source Center Document GMP20100534737006.

[15] Statement by Prime Minister Binyamin Netanyahu at the Prime Minister's Office in Jerusalem, Channel 10 Television, June 2, 2010, Open Source Center Document GMP 20100602738007.

[16] Ibid.

[17] Peter Spiegel, "Confrontation at Sea: Turkey Seeks U.S. Solidarity," *Wall Street Journal* (Europe), June 2, 2010.

[18] Turkish Ministry of Foreign Affairs, "Press Release Regarding the Use of Force by the Israeli Defense Forces Against the Humanitarian Aid Fleet to Gaza," Open Source Center Document GMP20100531017013, May 31, 2010.

[19] "Turkish Minister Speaks at the UN Security Council," (text) Anatolia, May 31, 2010, Open Source Center Document GMP20100601017001.

[20] Remarks to Justice and Development Party (AKP) parliamentary group, June 1, 2010, Anatolia, Open Source Center Document GMP20100601744001.

[21] Adem Kadam, "Prime Minister in Konya," Anatolia, June 4, 2010, Open Source Center Document GMP20100608734014.

[22] United Nations Security Council, S/PRST/2010/9, June 1, 2010.

[23] "British PM Tells Netanyahu Israeli Raid on Ship was 'Unacceptable'," Agence France Presse, June 1, 2010.

[24] "Merkel tells Israeli, Turkish Leaders of 'Deep Concern,'" Agence France Presse, May 31, 2010.

[25] "France's Sarkozy Wants Probe into Gaza Flotilla Incident," Agence France Presse, May 31, 2010.

[26] http://www.consilium.europa.eu/Newsroom.

[27] Ya'aqov Katz, "IDF Probe Considers Turkey Intel Needs," Jerusalem Post, June 14, 2010.

[28] Interview by Francesco Battistini, "The Only Mistake Lay in Underestimating the Pacifists," Milan *Corriere della Sera*, June 9, 2010, Open Source Center Document EUP 20100609058010.

[29] "Israel Announces Probe Commission with 2 Foreign Observers of 'Highest Standing,'" (Israeli) Government Press Office, June 13, 2010.

[30] "Statement by the Press Secretary on Israel's Investigation into Flotilla Incident," June 13, 2010, http://www.whitehouse.gov/the-press-office/statement-press-secretary-israels-investigation-flotilla-incident.

[31] "Turkey FM Says Ankara Entitled to Review Ties with Israel," Anatolia, June 14, 2010, BBC Monitoring Newsfile.

[32] "Turkey Said Distrustful of Israeli Probe," *Today's Zaman*, June 15, 2010.

[33] Yitzhaq Ben-Horn, "Baraq to ban: Trust Israel Flotilla Probe," Ynetnews, June 21, 2010.

[34] "Turkey Sets Up Committee to Look into Israeli Raid," Al-Manar TV Online, June 17, 2010

[35] Scott Wilson, Glenn Kessler, "U.S. Warned Israel Before Raid," *Washington Post*, June 3, 2010.

[36] Sheera Frenkel, "Israeli Battle with Pro-Palestinian Activists Endangers Peace Talks," McClatchy, May 31, 2010.

[37] U.S. Department of State, June 2, 2010.

[38] Isabel Kershner, Neil MacFarquhar, "Israel Begins Deporting Activists Held after Sea Raid," *New York Times*, June 3, 2010.

[39] "Erdogan to Obama: Israel Risks Losing its Best Friend in Middle East," June 3, 2010, http://www.haaretz.com.

[40] Statement made on PBS' "Charlie Rose Show," June 2, 2010, quoted in Wilson and Kessler, op.cit.

[41] The largest share or $240 million is in Overseas Private Investment Corporation (OPIC) mortgage financing for the West Bank. Another $75 million is FY2010 U.S. Agency for International Development (USAID) aid to support the PA's work to improve infrastructure

and $10 million to enhance private sector competitiveness in the West Bank and Gaza; it is unanswered how the PA will work in Gaza

[42] Remarks by President Obama and President Abbas of the Palestinian Authority after Meeting, June 9, 2010, http://www.whithouse.gov/the-press-office/remarks-president-

[43] "Hamas Rejects Israeli Proposal on Reopening Crossings," Al-Sharq al-Awsat website, June 4, 2010, BBC Monitoring Middle East.

[44] Communique issued by the Prime Minister's Media Adviser, Government Press Office, June 17, 2010, Open Source Center Document, GMP20100617746001.

[45] "Statement following the Israeli Security Cabinet Meeting," Prime Minister's Office, June 20, 2010, Open Source Center Document GMP20100620739004.

[46] Charles Levinson, "Israel Eases Gaza Blockade," *Wall Street Journal*, June 21, 2010.

[47] "Turkey Welcomes Ease of Gaza Blockade but Says not Enough," Anatolia, June 22, 2010.

[48] For text of Agreement, see http://www.israel-mfa.gov.il/MFA/Peace+ Process/ Reference+Documents/Agreed+documents+on+movement+and+access+from+and+to+Gaza+15-Nov-2005.htm.

[49] "Hamas Rejects Abbas Insistence on Supervising Gaza Aid," http://www.haaretz.com, June 14, 2010.

[50] "Paper Reports on Plans to Send Iranian, Lebanese Aid Ships to Gaza," Al-Sharq al-Awsat website, June 17, 2010, BBC Monitoring Middle East, June 18, 2010.

[51] Sabrina Tavernise, Michael Slackman, "Fatalities on Gaza Flotilla Said to Include U.S. Citizen," *New York Times*, June 3, 2010.

[52] Marc Champion, " Turkey Lashes out at Israel and Denounces 'Massacre'," *Wall Street Journal*, June 2, 2010.

[53] Umit Enginsoy, "Turkey's Military programs with Israel Remain in Place," http://www.hurriyetdailynews.com, June 3, 2010.

[54] "Turkey to Isolate Israel if International Probe Committee Not Set Up – Minister," Anatolia, June 9, 2010, BBC Monitoring European, June 10, 2010.

[55] "Israel's Attack Against Ship Taking Aid to Gaza," Anatolia (government news agency), Open Source Center Document GMP20100601744025.

[56] Mark Landler, "U.S. Tries to Keep its Balance between Turkey and Israel," *New York Times*, June 2, 2010.

INDEX

D

E

F

G

H

P

R

U

V

W